State, Revolution, and Superpowers in Afghanistan

State, Revolution, and Superpowers in Afghanistan

HAFIZULLAH EMADI

PRAEGER

New York
Westport, Connecticut
London

Library of Congress Cataloging-in-Publication Data

Emadi, Hafizullah.
    State, revolution, and superpowers in Afghanistan / Hafizullah
Emadi.
        p.   cm.
    Includes bibliographical references.
    ISBN 0-275-93460-8 (alk. paper)
        1. Afghanistan—Politics and government—1973–   2. Afghanistan—
Foreign relations—United States.   3. United States—Foreign
relations—Afghanistan.   4. Soviet Union—Foreign relations—
Afghanistan.   5. Afghanistan—Foreign relations—Soviet Union.
I. Title.
DS371.2.E48   1990
958.1'04—dc20   89-22853

Library of Congress Catalog Card Number: 89-22853
ISBN: 0-275-93460-8

First published in 1990

Praeger Publishers, One Madison Avenue, New York, NY 10010
A division of Greenwood Press, Inc.

Printed in the United States of America

The paper used in this book complies with the
Permanent Paper Standard issued by the National
Information Standards Organization (Z39.48-1984).

10 9 8 7 6 5 4 3 2 1

This book is dedicated to my mother, Sayed-Begum,
to the memory of my father, Mr. Afghan,
and to the people of Afghanistan

Contents

Tables

Preface

There are numerous books and articles written by scholars on Afghanistan's politics and society. Those which have been written by scholars from upper class backgrounds stress the role and leadership of this class in Afghanistan's development and modernization since the post–World War II period. Books that have been written by scholars of middle class backgrounds tend to analyze socioeconomic and political developments in Afghanistan from the perspective of the upper class in that country. Books written by foreign scholars remain descriptive of Afghanistan's march to modernity and development and lack a comprehensive analysis of socioeconomic and political contradictions in the country. The solution they prescribe does not differ significantly from development strategies pursued by the ruling class in Afghanistan.

The number of books written by scholars on Afghanistan and Afghan scholars in exile in the West increased following the Soviet military involvement in Afghanistan in December 1979. These books stress the Islamic character of Afghanistan and promote the establishment of an Islamic state in the country. This is more evident in the writings of Afghan scholars with upper middle class backgrounds and those associated with them who hope that by advancing Islamic ideology they would be able to secure leading positions in the future in Afghanistan.

Books written by scholars in the Soviet Union and its bloc, or scholars who are sympathetic toward Soviet-brand Marxism-Leninism and its political and philosophical orientation often try to show that the political change which occurred in Afghanistan in April 1978 is a "progressive" change intended to advance the interests of the oppressed people of the country. Furthermore, these works try to justify Soviet support of the state in Afghanistan and its nine years of military involvement in that country on the basis of "proletarian Internationalism" to defend the cliental state against external aggression of the Pakistan-based Islamic parties supported by the United States and other Western countries.

This book studies political developments in Afghanistan as a manifestation of the contention between two superpowers to expand their spheres of influence in Afghanistan. The main impetus leading me to start this book was the debate on how dependent development in peripheral societies led to alliances with the two superpowers—the United States and the Soviet Union—and how the latter, using their material resources, attempted to establish its domination over the former. As a member of the intellectual community and an active participant in the movement for progressive social transformation in Afghanistan, I was further encouraged to examine the validity of this debate by examining developments in that country. Thus the present work is a manifestation of my thirst for knowledge of social change in Afghanistan.

The epistemology that guides the analysis throughout the book is based on the discourse of a materialist interpretation of society—discourse which has been absent in writings of Afghanistan's history, politics, and social developments. The prime objective of this book is to reveal the modus operandi of superpower contention in Afghanistan and to gain a new understanding of how conflicts of interest among various factions of the ruling class within the state apparatus in an era of a capitalist world system results in superpower struggle for spheres of influence. I believe the book makes a modest contribution toward a better understanding of Afghanistan's politics and society.

Acknowledgments

This work is a summation of several years of reading, research, and observation of developments in Afghanistan in the era of superpower rivalry. The writing of this book would not have been possible without the assistance and support of various people both at academic institutions and in private business. Fearing that I might forget some person or institution, I am hesitant to begin. I am most deeply indebted to Professor Robert B. Stauffer, Department of Political Science, University of Hawaii-Manoa, for his exhaustive analysis and thoughtful advice concerning the final version of this book. I express my special appreciation to Professor Manfred Henningsen, Department of Political Science, University of Hawaii-Manoa, for providing both emotional support and intellectual stimulation in writing the book. This work was also enhanced by the special part played by Professors Glenn D. Paige, Yasumasa Kuroda and Assistant Professor Farideh Farhi, Department of Political Science, and Professor Jagdish P. Sharma, Department of History, University of Hawaii-Manoa.

My sincere thanks go to Mrs. Patricia A. Polansky, Bibliographer, Hamilton Library, University of Hawaii-Manoa, for her tireless assistance in locating materials and documents necessary for writing this book. I am particularly grateful to my wife Lorilei Emadi who consistently provided moral and material support during my research, translated some Russian documents on the subject and helped me in preparing an index for the book.

I owe special thanks to Professor Stephen P. Cohen, Department of Political Science, University of Illinois at Urbana-Champaign (on leave working in the Department of State, Washington, D.C. in 1986-87), for providing me an opportunity to use the Department of State library. I extend my gratitude to various individual Afghans in exile who provided me literature on socioeconomic and political developments in Afghanistan, and former U.S. ambassador to Afghanistan Mr. Theodore L. Eliot, Jr., for discussing with me U.S. politics in Afghanistan prior to the Soviet invasion of the country in December 1979. A very special acknowledgment is due the Institute of Culture and Communication, East-West Center, Honolulu, Hawaii, which allowed me the use of their facilities in preparing the final version of this book. Finally I would like to thank Praeger Publishers for bringing *State, Revolution, and Superpowers in Afghanistan* to the eyes of the world.

Introduction

The post–World War II era is considered to be a period of rapid development and modernization in Afghanistan. The political and social vicissitudes during the pre–World War II period in the country were characterized by (a) public disenchantment over slow socioeconomic development and oppressive administration compounded by the disquieting attitude of a great number of the intelligentsia of upper and middle class backgrounds within leadership positions, who considered themselves inferior vis-à-vis developed societies; and (b) the struggle and efforts by various progressive sociopolitical forces within the state apparatus to find solutions to resolve the country's underdevelopment.

The overabundance of literature that has been published on Afghanistan's modernization, development, and state formation in the past depicts Afghanistan as a tribal society and the state as an institution which serves the interests of all people regardless of their social and class affiliations (Richard Newell, *Politics of Afghanistan,* 1972; Louis Dupree, *Afghanistan,* 1973; Abdul Samad Ghaus, *The Fall of Afghanistan,* 1988, and others). Although the literature contains a well-documented description of events in the country, it lacks analysis of socioeconomic and political developments and fails to note the class-character of the state, the struggle among various social strata within the state, and the alliances that each social stratum formed with superpowers in order to establish and consolidate their base of power.

This book, in essence, studies the formation of the state and its role in the modernization and development of Afghanistan and examines how struggle among various socio-political forces within the state in Afghanistan led to alliances with superpowers. The study also explores how the United States and the Soviet Union tried to win Afghanistan to their respective spheres of influence, and how the Soviet Union, having failed to achieve its hegemonic building project around a class faction within the state apparatus in Afghanistan, resorted to the use of force and occupied the country in December 1979.

Primary data and documents concerning Afghanistan's national development strategies following World War II were used in this analysis as well as a number of secondary sources and documents on the subject. The primary sources that have been used in this research include (a) government documents, (b) documents published by scholars on Afghanistan and (c) materials published by political organizations both within and without Afghanistan.

Data materials published by the government of Afghanistan are the only original sources of documentation for most research on Afghanistan. To show steady progress and in order to draw international support for its needed development projects, the government tended to manipulate data such as demography, the state's accomplishments in economic and social progress, etc. This discrepancy has been remedied by contrasting the data with those of other governments and international organizations in order to get relatively accurate and reliable information.

Materials published on Afghanistan by scholars in the West are regarded as secondary sources. They are relatively reliable sources of information because most of the scholars lived in the country and directly experienced developments in Afghanistan. Other materials that were useful sources for analysis and which supplemented the existing information—information that could not be obtained from government archives because the government hid state-related information from the public for national or security reasons, or from other published materials—were documents published by political organizations in Afghanistan as well as abroad. In order to establish the reliability of some of the sources, efforts were made to link a survey of the literature with interviews of prominent scholars and politicians who are knowledgeable on Afghanistan's politics and society. Such an open-ended dialogic approach helped to avoid too much of a reliance on published materials; such reliance on literature alone would encourage acceptance of existing interpretations of developments and change in the country.

The structure of this book is as follows: the first chapter deals with the process of nation-state building in Afghanistan, studies sociopolitical stratifications in the country, and focuses on how various social strata within the state forged alliances with superpowers for material and political support to sponsor development strategies in Afghanistan. Chapter 2 studies modernization and development in Afghanistan following World War II and examines the role that the superpowers played in the fall of the monarchy in 1973. Chapter 3 examines the dialectical relations between internal and external factors that resulted in a military coup in 1978 and the establishment of a "democratic" state in Afghanistan; United States and Soviet relations during this period; and finally the Soviet involvement in Afghanistan's internal affairs in December 1979. Chapter 4 describes the various opposition political parties espousing different ideologies and examines the basis of the U.S. alliance with the Pakistan-based Islamic parties of Afghanistan. The last chapter attempts to synthesize the discussion and examines the future prospects of superpower struggle in Afghanistan.

1 State and Society

FORMATION OF A NATION-STATE

In the pre-independent period the state apparatus that developed in Afghanistan was weak and could not consolidate its authority throughout the country because it lacked popular support as well as a guiding ideology that would fuse it to civil society. The efficacy of the state was further reduced by feudal rivalries and colonial interventions. Although the rise and development of a modern state started in the mid-nineteenth century through a gradual expansion of the state bureaucracy, building of public schools, and inaugurating mass media for the purpose of cultivating popular obedience, the state still did not possess a national character.

The preliminary foundation for a nation-state was laid when Afghanistan gained its independence in 1919 under the leadership of King Amanullah. Amanullah was a young, progressive intellectual and a member of the movement agitating for Afghanistan's independence. Amanullah's espousal of nationalism helped him gain popularity among the discontented people. This situation on the one hand, and the establishment of a socialist system in Russia in October 1917 on the other, influenced King Amanullah and his associates to mobilize people in

Afghanistan for independence. On 3 April 1919 King Amanullah delivered a speech in which he addressed the nation stating: "I proclaim myself and my country completely free, independent and sovereign in all domestic and foreign issues. My country will thus become an independent state, just as other countries of the world."[1] Following this declaration, the British government launched its last major offensive on Afghanistan in May 1919 but was defeated and Afghanistan gained its independence.[2]

The Soviet Union was the first country to recognize Afghanistan's independence and sovereignty.[3] In a letter to King Amanullah, the Soviet government stated that it considered as void any imperialist treaty which the tsarist regime forced on the authorities in Afghanistan and would wholeheartedly return the occupied areas of Panjdeh and other regions to Afghanistan which had been seized by the tzarist regime in the nineteenth century. In October 1919, King Amanullah sent a delegate to Moscow to convey the message of the people of Afghanistan to the Soviet leadership. During a state banquet the delegate expressed Afghanistan's appreciation concerning the Soviet Union's policy of supporting anticolonial and national liberation struggles. The delegate assured the Soviet leadership that Afghanistan will follow the same objective in its foreign policy orientation and said, "we are certain that we can liberate the whole colonized people of the East with the help of the socialist Soviet Union."[4] The relationship between Afghanistan and the Soviet Union was further developed when the two countries exchanged diplomats at the ambassador level and concluded cultural, educational, and technical treaties on 28 February 1921.[5]

To expand Afghanistan's relations with other countries the state sent delegations to several European countries. As a result Britain recognized Afghanistan's independence in 1922; Germany in 1923. The relationship between Afghanistan and the Soviet Union grew stronger to the extent that the people of Afghanistan extended their support to the Soviet people when several Western countries tried to interfere in the Soviet Union's internal affairs by aiding internal opposition forces with the hope of toppling the revolutionary regime in that country. As many as 300 individual Afghans voluntarily went to the Soviet Union to support the Soviet people.

The strengthening of the relationship between Afghanistan and the Soviet Union was considered by the British as a major threat to its interests in the Indian subcontinent and it was because of this that the

British government continuously supported opposition forces in Afghanistan with the intention of overthrowing King Amanullah. The strengthening of a diplomatic relationship between Afghanistan and Germany and Germany's increasing participation in the former's development programs proved advantageous to the British. Although Britain regarded Germany as a main rival to its colonial expansionism, it welcomed Germany's active involvement in Afghanistan as a major factor in containing Soviet influence in that country as well as in the British colonies in South Asia.

In its foreign policy orientation the state supported freedom and independence movements in the Indian subcontinent by providing arms and ammunition, publishing anti-British pamphlets, and permitting several hundred Indian nationals and revolutionaries to settle in Afghanistan to conduct political activities for the liberation of their homeland. In 1921, an Indian Revolutionary government in exile was established and allowed to engage in political activities in Afghanistan. Mr. Raj Mahandra Partab, an Indian nationalist, was elected president and Mawlawai Barakatullah elected as prime minister with a 12 member cabinet.[6]

One of the major programs of the state was the modernization of the country. The state under the leadership of King Amanullah launched a plethora of political, social, and economic reforms. In 1923 the state promulgated the first constitution of Afghanistan. The constitution accorded equal status to all nationalities and individual citizens of the country, defined the rights of individual citizens and their relation to each other as well as to the state, and permitted the Shiite population of the country to freely practice their religious rituals without intimidation and harassment by individuals or public institutions. The constitution also abolished the practice of slavery and allowed non-Muslim national minorities (Hindus and Jews) to practice their religion and cultural traditions. To respect the Hindu nationals in Afghanistan the state also issued a decree encouraging the people not to sacrifice cows during the Muslim religious festivities because cows were considered to be sacred animals useful in primitive societies and their sacredness had been declared by Hindu religious authorities.[7] The state also introduced land reforms, restructured the tax system to finance the country's modernization program, and abolished *begari* (forced labor) except in the national services.

King Amanullah was fascinated by the cultural and social developments of European countries and tried to build a modern Afghanistan by mechanically emulating European developments into Afghanistan. To achieve this, King Amanullah introduced a number of social reforms which included complete emancipation of women, introduction of monogamy, compulsory education for both sexes, and separation of religion from politics and the state. In order to bring Afghanistan to the same level of social development similar to that of Europe, King Amanullah

sent Afghan girls abroad for higher education, opened girls schools and abolished the veil. Several high schools and many primary schools were established in different parts of the country. The teaching of French, and German, besides English, was also added to the curriculum. A large number of both sexes were sent abroad for higher education. Furthermore, inhabitants of Kabul and people visiting the capital were ordered to wear the European dress and hats.[8]

The state's radical policy of socioeconomic development (land reform, equal education, and modernization of higher educational institutions, etc.,) damaged the interests of many social strata within and outside the state apparatus, particularly those of feudal landowners and high officials who were also landowners.[9] Deprived of their privilege the feudal landowners and the highest religious circles (the Mujaddadi family, known as the Hazrat of Shorbazar, and the family of Shaikh Abdul Kadir Jailani, known as the Naqib Sahib) were engaged in instigating public opinion against the state under the pretext that the state violated Islamic law and the traditions of prophet Mohammad. The Mullahs' opposition to socioeconomic reform was not a manifestation of their religious prejudices, as many scholars of Afghanistan postulate, but rather an expression of their class interests because a great number of Mullahs either were landowners or were on their payrolls.[10]

The ensuing opposition by feudal landowners and conservative religious leaders also manifested itself in political struggle among state officials. The intensification of this struggle reduced the efficacy of the state to the extent that it could not respond to the complaints of the peasants concerning feudal exploitation and those of the disadvantaged social strata against the tyranny of some of the state officials who supported feudal landowners.[11] Officials within the state apparatus were divided into two sections: those who were proreform and those who were antireform.

The proreform groups concentrated around King Amanullah and favored heavy taxation to finance the country's modernization program. Decrees were issued concerning restructuring of the tax system and the collection of state revenues. Implementation of the decrees caused tremendous suffering and anger among the poor peasants and farmers. They submitted applications to the state requesting a reduction in taxes. Instead of alleviating the burden of the peasantry King Amanullah further increased taxation to support his ambitious modernization projects. Amanullah's negligence of the deteriorating social conditions of the peasantry on the one hand, and the opposition within the state on the other, provided feudal landowners and religious clerics, supported by the British government, the opportunity for antistate propaganda. This situation paved the way for rebellion against the state in a few regions. It was in January 1929 that Habibullah, known by the name of Bache-e-Saqaw (the water carrier's son) from Kohdaman, organized a group of armed men and launched a major assault on the capital, Kabul, to overthrow King Amanullah and establish an Islamic state in the country. King Amanullah fled to Kandahar and then to Italy. He did not fight because he believed that resistance would ruin the country and bring disaster to the nation.[12]

After the seizure of state on 23 May 1929 Habibullah took the appellation of Khadim-e-dini Rasul-u-llah (the servant of the faith of the prophet) and was supported by people in Kohdaman (his native home), the Pushtun tribes of Ghilzais, and a number of religious clerics and feudal landowners. Although the British were happy with the abdication of King Amanullah, they were not pleased with Habibullah as the new king of Afghanistan. He was illiterate, lacked charisma, and was unable to effectively protect British interests.

Habibullah's short rule collapsed because he could not offer a policy of social development that would appeal to a wide spectrum of the population nor was he in a position to consolidate his rule in the country, particularly in frontier tribal regions, the Hazarajat, and other provinces which were still loyal to King Amanullah. This situation paved the way for his downfall on 8 October 1929 after a nine-month rule. The resistance was led by General Mohammad Nadir and his four brothers. General Nadir did not enjoy popular support, so he mobilized people of the frontier areas against Habibullah on the pretext of securing the throne for King Amanullah. For this reason General Nadir was supported by Pushtun tribes from Paktiya province, the Waziri tribes, and the people in Kabul to overthrow Habibullah. The British government also supported General Nadir because the British considered him an astute politician who could not only reduce the Soviet influence in Afghanistan but could also strengthen the country's ties with Britain.

When General Nadir captured the capital, Kabul, Habibullah fled to Kuhistan, Parwan province and established his base there. Nadir sent his envoy to Habibullah to attempt to convince him to come to Kabul, asking Habibullah to meet with him and discuss who should be the king. Habibullah did not trust Nadir and demanded some kind of guarantee from him. Nadir wrote a note on the margin of the Quran, a holy book, to the effect that he promised not to do any harm to Habibullah if he came to Kabul. Nadir signed the note and put his seal on it and sent the Quran to Habibullah.[13] This was enough to convince Habibullah and he came to Kabul. Upon his arrival in Kabul he was arrested and soon executed.

After Habibullah's execution General Nadir proclaimed himself the new king of Afghanistan. In most parts of the country the people were not happy with King Nadir when they found that he deceived them when, to gain their support, he promised to restore King Amanullah to the throne. The Pushtun tribes of Shinwar, Wazir, and others revolted against him in favor of King Amanullah. King Nadir successfully put down the rebellion by bribing the tribal heads of these communities. When the people in Parwan and other parts of the country defied King Nadir's rule and rebelled against him, King Nadir used his Pushtun tribes to retaliate against them with such brutality that the memory of it still haunts people in the country, particularly the people of Parwan province.

To legitimize the state and his rule as head of state King Nadir promoted Islam as a state religion. He distinguished this policy from the similar ploy adopted by Habibullah, that is, to use Islam to draw the people behind him, by portraying Habibullah as a bandit of Tadjik background who seized the throne from the Pushtuns.[14] After consolidating his base of power King Nadir strengthened Afghanistan's relations with Britain and received substantial amounts of financial and military assistance from the British government. This enabled him to equip a modern standing army and maintain stability in the country.[15]

With the coming to power of Nadir as a monarch, British and German participation increased in Afghanistan's development projects. The leadership in Afghanistan later saw Germany as a rising power and tried to strengthen its relations with it so as to be able to rely on Germany not only in case of interference by other major powers in the country's internal affairs but also against internal opposition forces who might challenge the leadership. The pro-German elites within the state apparatus asked Germany to help Afghanistan with her development projects. Germany became a dominant influence in Afghanistan until the outbreak of World War II. According to Ludwig Adamec "the Germany of the Third Reich was more acceptable than the Weimar Republic because the ruling class considered it as an implacable foe of the Soviets."[16]

In 1930 King Nadir called a *Loya Jirgah* (Grand Assembly of tribal leaders) to endorse the new constitution of Afghanistan and to confirm him as king of Afghanistan. Aside from defining the obligations of the king, it specifically justified Nadir's rule, claiming that he was responsible for achieving independence for Afghanistan and its people. It further stipulated that all future kings of Afghanistan must be of Pushtun background and of the Hanifi school of Islam. In order to "Islamicize" the state apparatus, the Loya Jirgah and King Nadir decreed that subsequent kings must swear a particular oath in the house of the *Majlis-e-Shura* (National Consultative Assembly):

I swear by Almighty God and the sacred Quran, knowing that God the Glorious is omnipresent and omniscient, to rule according to the Shariat of Mohammad and the fundamental rules of the country (and to strive) for the protection of the glorious religion of Islam, the independence of Afghanistan and the rights of the nation, and for the defense, progress and prosperity of the country. So help me God through the blessings of the sacred spiritual force of the blessed saints (the approval of God be upon them).[17]

Having consolidated his sociopolitical base of power King Nadir went on to outline the state's policies:

My government will use the Islamic law and principles as a guiding light and will take necessary measures to implement the Shariat and prohibit alcoholic beverage, to establish a military school and an arsenal for the manufacturing of modern weapons, maintain diplomatic relations with foreign powers, repair telegraphs and telephones, improve roads, collect arrears of public revenue, develop commercial relations with foreign powers, advance public instruction and finally to reconstruct the old Council of State and appoint a Prime Mnister who would form a cabinet subject to the royal approval.[18]

To get religious leaders firmly behind him King Nadir created the *Jamiat ul Ulama* (Society of Islamic Scholars) and removed the restrictions and limitations on social, political, and educational works that King Amanullah had imposed upon religious leaders. He was responsible for Afghanistan's first printed version of the Quran which had formally appeared only in handwritten form or were foreign imports. He formalized the Sunni school of Islam—Afghanistan's official relgion—declared the inequality of men and women, closed down all girls schools throughout the country, and reinvoked the veil for women. He repayed some members of the influential Hazrat family of Shorbazar district, Kabul, by appointing them to high government posts.

Since King Nadir seized state and political power with the help of the Pushtun tribes of Paktiya and those of the frontier regions, he exempted them from paying taxes and from serving in the armed forces. King Nadir relied on these Pushtun tribes for the maintenance and consolidation of his rule and appointed Pushtun bureaucrats to administer daily affairs in the non-Pushtun regions. He pursued a policy of "divide and conquer," pitting one nationality against the other to perpetuate their instability and to prevent them from organizing an uprising against him.

In 1933 King Nadir was assassinated by a supporter of former King Amanullah. King Nadir's young son Mohammad Zahir succeeded him and served as a figurehead ruler, while the administering of power was handled by his uncles, Prime Ministers Mohammad Hashim (1930–1946), and Shah Mahmood (1946-1953). Under their leadership, the state modernized and equipped the army and police forces, not only for the purpose of defending the country against foreign intervention but also for suppressing opposition and internal resistance.[19] They also expanded the state apparatus by opening new departments:

In 1931 Afghanistan had a Prime Ministry, a Ministry of War, Ministry of Foreign Affairs, Ministry of Interior, Ministry of Justice, Ministry of Finance, Ministry of Trade, Ministry of Education and the Independent Directorate of Health, Post and Telegraph, while in post-World War II era, there were the Ministries of Public Works, of Mines and Industries, of Agriculture, of Communication, of Public Health and the Department of Press and that of Tribal Affairs.[20]

Having achieved political stability and expanded the bureaucracy, the state was now ready to modernize the educational system with the hope of creating a new generation of administrators who could fuse a close link between the state and civil society. To this end, the state adopted some elements of Western education. This Westernization trend gradually increased and teachers were brought in from the United States, Britain, and Australia.[21]

The primary concern of the state in modernizing and developing education was to promote a national ideology. Prime Minister Mohammad Hashim expressed his views on this subject: "We must transform the thoughts of the Afghans before we can build an ultra-Western capital, as Amanullah tried to do. He saw only the outward forms of Modernization."[22] The policy of building a national ideology for the state was formulated early in 1936, when the state tried to declare Pushtu the official language of the country. Prime Minister Mohammad Hashim, during an interview in 1937, said "from next year it [Pushtu] is to become the language of our officials, doing away with Persian. Our legends and our poems will then be understood by everyone. We shall draw from them a pride in our culture of the past which will unite us."[23]

This hegemonic national project fully materialized in 1950 when for the first time a law was passed that made Pushtu the official means of communication. According to this law

the government employees were forced to speak and write correspondences in Pushtu. . . . The Ministry of Education under the leadership of Mohammad Naim, the brother of Prime Minister Mohammad Daoud (1953-1963) took the responsibility of publishing books to promote the Pushtu language. In addition to this, several other institutions were established to promote this cause. Names of places were changed from Persian to Pushtu in all Persian and non-Pushtu speaking areas. . . . It was during this rising tide of Pushtun nationalism that King Zahir nicknamed one of his sons, Mohammad Daoud, Pushtunyar [Friend of the Pushtun].[24]

The Pushtu Tulana Institute was established to conduct research in the Pushtu language, culture, and traditions and to use this research toward the state goal of "Pushtunization" of the country's cultural, political, and social life. To further establish the domination of Pushtun culture the state, under the leadership of King Zahir, extended its support to Pushtun tribal chiefs, influential landowners, and big businessmen to draw their support, and sponsored various economic and industrial development projects in most Pushtun-settled areas. The main goal was to make Pushtuns symbols of progress to the people and to make their culture more acceptable to non-Pushtuns.

The effects of World War II were felt in Afghanistan. The country initially adopted a "wait and see" attitude regarding the Allies and the Axis powers, fearing possible damage to their own internal stability. World War II, and its eventual impact on Afghanistan in the form of termination of financial and technical aid for their development projects, meant that Afghanistan's modernization program was stalled. During the war both the Soviet Union and Britain were suspicious of the Afghan-German relationship and the presence of a large number of German technical experts in that country. When the British asked the leadership in Afghanistan to declare the country's position regarding the war, they declared the country's neutrality. Then the British pressed Afghanistan to expel all German nationals and experts from the country. Afghanistan's leaders had no other option but to comply with the British demand. With Germany's defeat at the end of the war, its role as a major power ended in the country. The ruling class in Afghanistan then tried to strengthen the country's relationships with the United States, which had emerged victorious from the war.[25] Although the United States established its mission in Kabul on June 6, 1942, in the immediate post-war years the United States increased its participation in Afghanistan's development and provided economic assistance to finance the country's agricultural projects.

The development and transformation of the Soviet Union as a major power in world politics in the late 1950s also influenced developments in Afghanistan. A section of the merchant and bureaucratic bourgeoisie that benefited from trading with the Soviet Union began to expand trade with the Soviet Union and its bloc. The expanding of economic, cultural, and political ties with the two major powers of the time, the United States and the Soviet Union, in the 1960s divided the bourgeoisie in the country. Merchant and bureaucratic bourgeoisie and intellectuals associated with the ruling class within the state apparatus developed either pro-U.S. or pro-Soviet tendencies in their socio-political orientations.

In order to give the state a "democratic" shield, the ruling class under the leadership of King Zahir introduced a new constitution in 1963. The constitution barred immediate members of King Zahir's family from participation in the government,[26] accorded the Persian language equal status to Pushtu, and nominally allowed the establishment of political parties. On the basis of the constitution Mohammad Daoud, King Zahir's cousin, was forced to resign from the post of premiership and Dr. Mohammad Yusuf was appointed prime minister in his place. The prime objective of the ruling class was, on the one hand, to expand the social base of the monarchy and, on the other, to look for excuses to attribute any mishandling and mismanagement of the country's socioeconomic and political development to the prime ministers.

During the constitutional period (1963-1973) four prime ministers were appointed, one after the other, but none actually succeeded in improving the lots of the overwhelming majority of the people. The economic, political, and social crises that encapsulated the country on the one hand, and the struggle of various social strata within the state apparatus on the other, hastened the crisis of legitimation of the state. This situation finally paved the way for the takeover of state by another section of the ruling class, which was concentrated around former Premier Mohammad Daoud, and the proclamation of Afghanistan as a republic in 1973.

Although the ruling class succeeded in establishing a modern state (a modern army, the police, expanding the bureaucracy, inaugurating modern schools to educate new cadres of administrators, etc.,) and portrayed it as a national institution that serves the interest of all classes, the state remained an instrument of class oppression. The development strategies that those in the leadership position articulated did not go beyond their narrow class interests. As a result the ruling class within and outside the state apparatus alienated itself from civil society because: (a) it did not permit members of the middle and lower classes to assume leadership positions in the state apparatus and (b) it monopolized key economic and industrial enterprises as well as import-export activities. Lacking both popular support and financial resources for development and modernization, the leadership in Afghanistan relied on foreign companies and governments and allowed them to invest capital in Afghanistan. Such a trend of development blocked the growth of the national bourgeoisie and relegated the existing ones into subordinate positions from which they could not consolidate themselves and provide leadership for the country.

SOCIAL STRATIFICATION

Afghanistan is considered to be one of the most backward and underdeveloped societies in the capitalist world economy. Modernization and

Table 1.1
Ethnolinguistic Communities in Afghanistan (in millions)

Ethnic Group	Language	Religious Sect	Number
Pushtun	Pushtu	Sunni (a few Shiite)	6.5
Tadjik	Persian	Sunni, Shiite and Ismaili in the Northeast	4.1
Hazara	Persian	Shiite, Ismaili and Sunni	1.0
Uzbek	Uzbeki	Sunni	1.0
Aimaq	Persian (some Turkic words)		
Brahui	Brahui (Dravidian)	Sunni	.8
Turkmen	Turkic Dialects	Sunni	.2
Baluch	Baluchi	Sunni	.2
Nuristani	"Kafiri" (Indo-European)		.1
Pamiris	Indo-Iranian dialects	Sunni	.1
		Sunni and Ismaili	a few 1000s

Kohistani	Dardic dialects	Sunni	a few 1000s
Gujar	Indo-European dialects (Pushtu)	Sunni	a few 1000s
Qirghiz	Turkic	Sunni	a few 1000s
Jat	Indo-European dialects (Pushtu)	Sunni	a few 100s
Arab	Persian	Sunni	a few 100s
Mongol	Persian (with some Mongol words)	Sunni	a few 100s
Hindu	Speaks Persian and Pushtu (Mother tongue is either Hindi or Punjabi)	Hinduism	20,000
Sikh	Speaks Persian and Pushtu (Mother tongue is either Hindi or Punjabi)	Sikhism	10,000
Jews (Yahud)	All speak Persian and Pushtu (Mother tongue is Hebrew)	Judaism	a few 100s

Source: Robert L. Canfield, "Ethnic, Regional and Sectarian Alignments in Afghanistan," in *The State, Religion and Ethnic Politics: Afghanistan, Iran and Pakistan*, ed. Ali Banuazizi and Myron Weiner (New York: Syracuse University Press, 1986), p. 78.

capitalist development occurred unevenly in different parts of the country. In some regions this process occurred rapidly, in others very slowly, while in some remote areas of the country the communal tribal system remained intact. This was because of the country's lack of resources for development and lack of communication and trade links among various regions caused by rugged mountains and the harsh climate. This uneven socioeconomic and political development was compounded by ensuing struggle among various national (ethnic) communities, particularly tensions between the upper strata of the politically dominant nationality (the Pushtuns) and the national (ethnic) minorities. Tension between various national communities was further aggravated by religious differences among the Sunnites, Shiites, and the Ismailites (a subbranch of the Shiite sect).

The state strategies of socio-political developments, for example, the practice of Pushtun favoritism, the concentration of economic development projects in Pushtun areas, and the appointment of Pushtuns to top administrative posts in non-Pushtun areas added more fuel to national tensions and antagonized national minorities, particularly the Tadjiks, Uzbeks, and Turkmen in the north, and the Hazaras in the central part of the country, against the ruling class in Afghanistan. Their hostility grew when the state enacted a new constitution in 1964 which institutionalized the Sunni sect of Islam and stipulated that the king should be a follower of the Hanifi school of Islam (article 8).[27] Table 1.1 shows various national communities that make up the mosaic of Afghanistan's social structure.

The overwhelming majority of the population is engaged in agricultural activities but with the gradual integration of Afghanistan into the capitalist world economy the country's economically active population can be classified as follows:

The feudals

The peasants

The bourgeoisie

The technocratic and bureaucratic elites

The working class

The Feudals

The consolidation of feudal authority which began during the last third of the nineteenth century led to the establishment of a strong central government in Afghanistan. Such a consolidation of power was not only the result of economic development (the growth of cities, development of trade, and business which demanded a strong government to eliminate feudal warfare and peasant uprisings), but was also due to the necessity of organizing popular resistance to colonial interventions in the country's internal affairs, particularly the British colonial government.[28]

The process of centralization of political power was further accomplished during the reign of King Abd-al-Rahman in 1880-1901. Although feudal landowners recognized the central government, they continued to exercise their power and influence in their respective communities. Shortly after the country's independence in 1919 the state tried to restrict the authority of the feudal landowners in the administration of the country. Facing severe opposition by feudal landowners and religious clerics associated with them, the state collapsed in 1929. Since then feudal landowners remained an important element of social power in the rural areas. Their influence was so pervasive that state officials were unable to collect taxes, recruit soldiers, etc., without their cooperation.

Feudal landowners influenced social politics in rural areas not only due to their economic position but also because of their association with religious leaders, the Mullahs. Since most Mullahs in Afghanistan were on the payrolls of feudal landowners, they played a major role in consolidating the power of feudal landowners. Because Mullahs were in charge of performing religious ceremonies, they were in a position to make people believe in the authority of feudal landowners. People were told that unless they obey and repay their debts to feudal landowners— the local chiefs—they will not be permitted to enter heaven after their death. In return for the services the Mullahs rendered feudal landowners, the latter set aside a piece of communal land for them, and Mullahs became part of the feudal system in the country.

According to government statistics of 1978 there are 7.91 million hectares of arable land in Afghanistan (3.75 million hectares of land under temporary crops, 0.14 million hectares of land under permanent crops, 4.02 million hectares of uncultivated land) and 54.7 million hectares of permanent pastures and meadows. Thus, the total area of

Table 1.2

Distribution of Landholdings among Landowners, 1978

Size of Landholding 43,827,000 Hectares (70% of all lands)	No. of Landowners	Percentage of Landowners
2.02—4.05 Hectares	1,084,824	83
4.05—10.12 Hectares	156,842	12
10.12—20,242.9 Hectares	65,351	5
	1,307,017	100

Source: Saleh Mohammad Zeray, *Kabul Times*, 15 September 1978.

agricultural land does not exceed 62.61 million hectares.[29] Before the military coup in 1978 there were 1,307,017 families of all categories of landowners who possessed 70 percent of all agricultural land.[30]

Recent statistics indicate that 83 percent of landowners possessed between 2.02 to 4.05 hectares of fertile land and 12 percent of landowners hold 4.05 to 10.12 hectares of agricultural land. At the top of this pyramid there were five percent of feudal landowners who possessed between 10.12 to 20,242.9 hectares of the most fertile agricultural land (see Table 1.2).

The Peasants

According to 1978 government statistics, out of Afghanistan's total population of 15.108 million there are 10,839,087 peasants engaged in agricultural activities.[31] Approximately 70 percent of all agricultural land—43,827,000 hectares—belonged to landowners, important officials, and merchants. It is estimated that approximately 13 percent of the agricultural land—8,139,300 hectares—belongs to the state and religious clerics, leaving 17 percent—10,643,700 hectares—to the peasants. Roughly 70 percent of all peasants remain landless and work as agricultural laborers or sharecroppers. Ten percent of cultivated land belongs to middle and well-to-do peasants, who possess two to six hectare plots, yet they constitute only six percent of the total number of peasant-landowners. The remaining seven percent of cultivated land is divided among 24 percent of peasant-landowners, who possess one to two hectare plots (see Table 1.3).

The majority of peasants are tenant farmers dependent on feudal landowners. Various types of leases exist in the country based on who provides the land, capital, water, seed, and labor. For example, if the landowner provides the land, capital, water, and the seed, he takes four-fifths of the harvest and the tenant gets only one-fifth. If the tenant provides capital and seed he receives two-fifths of the harvest. The tenant must also provide service to the landowners such as repairing roads, cleaning ditches, and household duties, etc.

The peasants, in addition to working on the lands of feudal land-owners, also pay different kinds of taxes to the state and clandestine surcharges to the tax collectors. Such severe living conditions and grueling exploitation resulted in periodic peasant uprisings in different parts of the country and the migration of landless and poor peasants to cities in search of employment.[32]

The Bourgeoisie

The introduction of a capitalist mode of production in Afghanistan began during the reign of King Shir Ali in 1868–1879, when the process of world capitalist development was finding its way eastward through colonial powers of the period. The internal stability achieved at that time provided an opportunity for the inauguration of a few light industries such as arms manufacturing, postal services, and others.[33] The bourgeois class that emerged out of feudalism was relatively weak and not in a position to play a significant role in the transformation of socioeconomic development in the country.

The process of industrialization was intensified during King Abd-al-Rahman's reign (1880–1901) and his son's, King Habibullah (1901–1919). The state needed arms and other war-related supplies and supported the development of industries producing paramilitary and non-military products. As a result several industries such as arms manufacturing, boot making, coin minting, leather, and textiles had been established. There also developed a large-scale, lucrative government monopoly for the manufacture of wine, whiskey, and brandy for export.[34] Later a unit of the electrical network with a capacity of 15,000 KW was installed in Jabul Seraj, 80 km north of Kabul to facilitate the process of further industrial development.[35]

Table 1.3
Distribution of Landholdings among Peasants, 1978

Hectares of Land	No. of Peasants	% of Landholding	% of Peasants
6,261,000	650,345	10	6
4,382,700	2,601,381	7	24
—	7,587,361	—	70
10,643,700	10,839,087	17	100

Sources: Vladimir Glukhoded, ''Economy of Independent Afghanistan,'' in *Afghanistan: Past and Present* (Moscow: USSR Academy of Sciences, Oriental Studies in the USSR, no. 3, 1981), p. 242. Ministry of Planning, *Afghan Agriculture in Figures* (Kabul: Government Printing House, December, 1978).

Following the country's independence in 1919 the growth of the national bourgeoisie accelerated on practical grounds (the inauguration of several new factories such as match and printing industries, etc.) and ideological grounds through the inauguration of schools and newspapers (advancing bourgeois-democratic ideas). The state under the leadership of King Amanullah encouraged trade and private investment, and the state facilitated this through subsidizing private industries and selling state land to private individuals. The state's industrialization program was aimed at investment of internal capital in productive industries. As internal and external trade expanded there developed an increased managerial bureaucracy in the state sector and a national bourgeoisie in the private sector.[36]

The post-Amanullah period marks the beginning of state intervention in economic development in Afghanistan. In 1932 a state-owned bank, the National Bank of Afghanistan was established. After a few years of operation the bank monopolized all industrial establishments. Among the industries they controlled were cotton and woolen textiles, ceramics, sugar beets, soap, matches, canning plants, tanneries, and a metal foundry.[37] The financial institution's joint stock companies and subsidiaries controlled about 80 percent of the export-import trade.

Although the state established its control over key economic and industrial enterprises, it allowed the existence of small-scale private entrepreneurs. As a result of this policy a group of private investors established a commercial bank, the De Afghanistan Bank in 1939. The bank soon monopolized all financial transactions in the country.[38] In the post–World War II period the state further liberalized its economic policy and permitted private and foreign investors to invest capital in Afghanistan. To this end the state passed a new investment law bill. The advantages offered by the new investment law included

a five year tax holiday, duty free imports of capital goods and raw materials. Investors (were) also exempted from personal income tax and corporation tax and dividends for the first five years. . . . No export duties (were to) be levied on the export output of approved projects. Foreign personnel of approved enterprises (were) allowed to repatriate seventy percent of their income, net of taxes.[39]

As a result several private banks were established in the late 1960s which included the Pashtani Tejarati Bank, the Mortgage and Construc-

Table 1.4
Private Industries in Afghanistan, 1967

Type	No. of Industry	No. of Workers
Food Industry		
Raisin Processing, Casings, Rose Essence, Meat	14	657
Light Industry		
Textiles	20	2,467
Printing Press	2	36
Drugs	1	5
Service		
Garage	1	8
Dry Cleaning	4	123
Manufacturing		
Metals	6	121
Total	48	3,417

Source: *Afghanistan Industrial Development Project*, Checchi and Co. Final Report (Washington, D.C. and Kabul, September 1974).

tion Bank, the Industrial Development Bank, and the Agricultural Bank. Since the new law provided a profitable opportunity to foreign investors, a number of foreign-based corporations such as International Corporation, National Westminister Bank, First National City Bank, Chase Manhattan Bank, and overseas subsidiaries of several other corporations invested in Afghanistan and bought shares in the newly established banks.[40]

This trend of economic development led to a gradual increase in the growth of private industries throughout the country. Since the state monopolized heavy industries such as mines, gas, oil, etc., private entrepreneurs concentrated their investment in consumer branches of the national economy. Table 1.4 shows the number of private industries in Afghanistan in 1967.

Table 1.5
Composition of the White-Collar Workers, 1982

Type of Profession	No. of Workers	Percentage
Professional, technical related workers	98,674	2.5
Administrative managerial workers	8,027	0.2
Clerical related workers	86,394	2.2
Sales Workers	146,075	3.7
Service Workers	77,826	2.0
Total	416,996	10.6

Source: International Labour Organization (ILO), *Yearbook of Labour Statistics* (Geneva: 1982), p. 52.

THE BUREAUCRATIC AND TECHNOCRATIC ELITES

The capitalist mode of production and the influx of foreign economic aid to Afghanistan after World War II created a cadre of professional white-collar workers to serve as perpetuators of the state apparatus. These strata of workers come mainly from among upper and middle class backgrounds. Religious and ethnic affiliations played an important role in the selection of personnel for government posts—the top government administrative posts such as cabinet members, judges, governorships, etc., remained a monopoly of the elite of upper class backgrounds, mostly of Pushtun nationality. Intellectuals of other ethnic communities employed in various departments within the state apparatus (excluding the Ministry of Foreign Affairs), were not promoted beyond the rank of colonel in the army or director in a civil service department.

The expansion of educational institutions following the World War II period provided opportunities to national minorities to acquire a modern education. Their numbers increased in subsequent years, and their education, instead of cultivating proestablishment sentiments, made them more aware of their minority status among the Pushtun majority. In school they studied history and learned more about how preceding

Table 1.6
List of State-owned Industries, 1966

Type	No. of Industry	No. of Workers
Building Materials		
Cement, Tiles, Marble, etc.	11	2,500
Food Industry		
Flour Mills, Raisin Processing, Dried Fruits, etc.	12	1,500
Cotton Ginning and Vegetables		
Oil Mills	14	4,000
Manufacturing Industry		
Leather and Shoe	4	600
Chemicals, Plastics, Ceramics	7	200
Woodworking	6	670
Metal Construction, Motor Repair, etc.	13	3,000
Textiles	18	9,000
Total	85	21,470

Source: Afghanistan Industrial Development Project, Checchi and Co. Final Report (Washington, D.C. and Kabul, September 1974).

generations had been manipulated by the Pushtun leaderships. They were exposed to various political and philosophical currents, some of which accentuated their ethnolinguistic and regional differences, and gradually they began to voice their demands for the right to self-determination and the establishment of a separate nation.[41]

In order to deflect this growing trend among the intellectuals of national minorities and its impact on their communities, the state appointed two educated elites of Hazara nationality and one of Uzbek nationality as ministers of planning, mines, and commerce during the constitutional period (1963–1973). Their roles as ministers within the cabinet, however, were largely ceremonial.

Most intellectuals of upper and middle class backgrounds acquired

STATE AND SOCIETY 23

Table 1.7
Composition of Blue-Collar Workers, 1982

Industries	No. of Workers	Percentage of Workers
Manufacturing	423,373	10.7
Electric, Gas and Water	11,354	0.3
Construction	51,086	1.3
Mining & Quarrying	59,339	1.5
Total	545,152	13.8

Source: International Labour Organization (ILO), *Yearbook of Labour Statistics* (Geneva: 1982), p. 52.

their higher education in the West or in the Soviet Union and its bloc. These intellectuals also held important positions in private sectors of the country's economy. According to International Labour Organization (ILO) statistics, the salaried petty-bourgeoisie (white-collar workers), which include professionals, technical workers, and administrative managers, does not exceed 2.7 percent. If one includes service, clerical, and sales workers in this category, the number will reach 10.6 percent. Table 1.5 shows the make up of the white-collar workers in 1982.

The political role of the petty-bourgeois strata was contradictory over time due to tremendous oscillations. Sometimes they played an active role in the antiestablishment movements while other times they were the bulwark of reaction and part of the establishment.

THE WORKING CLASS

The preliminary foundation of small-scale industry (guns and artillery) which was laid down during the reign of King Shir Ali between 1869 and 1879, brought with it a new class in Afghanistan—the working class. During the reigns of his successors the numbers of blue-collar workers increased parallel to the increase in the number of industrial establishments. The process of industrialization developed very slowly prior to Afghanistan's independence in 1919. Subsequently a relative increase occurred in the establishment of industries so that by 1966, 85

Table 1.8
Social Divisions in Afghanistan

Class	Numbers	Members	Ethnic Affiliations
Elites	3,000	Senior state officials (military, police and civil service), clerics, wealthy businessmen, tribal chiefs and ethnic leaders	Mainly Pushtuns but a few from other nationalities
Intelligentsia	30,000	Junior level state employees, teachers, students, literati and artists, junior military and police officers	Mainly Pushtuns, with a small number of minority groups
Urban Middle Class	934,744	Lower level state employees (military, police and civil service), shopkeepers, artisans, religious leaders, merchants, etc.	All ethnic groups, but Pushtuns are growing in number

Blue-Collar Workforce	545,152	Skilled and semiskilled workers and servants	Mainly minority groups, but Pushtuns are growing in number
Landowners	1,307,017	All ethnic groups	All ethnic groups
Peasants	10,839,087	All ethnic groups	All ethnic groups
Nomads	1,449,000	—	Pushtuns
Total	15,108,000		

Sources: Ministry of Planning, *Afghan Agriculture in Figures* (Kabul: Government Printing House, 1978); International Labour Organization (ILO), *Yearbook of Labour Statistics* (Geneva: 1982).

industrial complexes existed which employed approximately 21,470 workers.

The number of state-owned industries increased in subsequent years (see Table 1.6). Several major industrial plants such as the Balkh and Bagrami Textile mills and the Nitrogen Fertilizer Factory in Balkh province had been established. The *Quarterly Economic Review,* quoting Afghanistan sources, indicates that by the early 1980s, more than 200 industrial projects had been built, or were under construction.[42] The ILO statistics of 1982 indicate that the number of workers in different industrial establishments was 545,152 or 13.8 percent of the population. Table 1.7 shows the number of blue-collar workers in 1982.

Although the blue-collar workers are small in their size compared to other social classes, their role in the country's economic development is considered to be of great significance. Since the post–World War II period the blue-collar workers have been active participants in the country's socioeconomic development. Yet their struggle did not meet with complete success as they could not develop their economic struggle (demand for pay raise, etc.) to the political struggle—the struggle for a new democratic society. Thus the blue-collar workers could not transform themselves from the position of subordination to that of domination. The bureaucratic bourgeoisie (some linked with land) and feudal landowners remained at the top of the country's social ladder. The elite associated with them held important positions within the state apparatus since the country's independence in 1919. Table 1.8 lists social classes, their numbers and ethnic affiliations.

NOTES

1. Naftula Khalfin, "The Struggle of the Peoples of Afghanistan for Independence and Against the British Colonialists," in *Afghanistan: Past and Present* (Moscow: Academy of Sciences, Oriental Studies in the USSR, no. 3, 1981), p. 113.

2. Ghulam Mohammad Ghubar, *Afghanistan dar Masir-e-Tarikh* [Afghanistan in the path of history] (Kabul: Government Printing House, 1967).

3. Naftula Khalfin, op. cit., p. 115.

4. Surkha (Sazmani Rahayi Bakhshi Khalqa-e-Afghanistan or Organization for Liberation of the People of Afghanistan), *Chegunagi-e- Paidayish wa Rushdi Bourgeoisie dar Afghanistan* [The process and development of bourgeoisie in Afghanistan] (Kabul: Ayendagan Press, 1980).

5. Yu V. Gankovsky et al., *A History of Afghanistan* (Moscow: Progress Publishers, 1982), p. 212.

6. Anand Gupta, *Lenin and India* (New Delhi: New Literatures, 1980).

7. Ghulam Mohammad Ghubar, op. cit., p. 231.

8. F. R. Farid, "The Modernization of Afghanistan," *Afghanistan* 17 (July-August-September 1962):15.

9. Naftula Khalfin, op. cit., p. 136.

10. Ghulam Mohammad Ghubar, op. cit., p. 231.

11. Ibid., pp. 801–6.

12. Surkha, op. cit., p. 30.

13. This information has not been cited in any of the existing literature on Afghanistan. The author gathered it through discussion with people who witnessed the event.

14. Ludwig W. Adamec, *Afghanistan's Foreign Affairs to the Mid-Twentieth Century* (Tucson: The University of Arizona Press, 1974), pp. 177–78.

15. Vartan Gregorian, *The Emergence of Modern Afghanistan: Politics of Reform and Modernization* (Palo Alto: Stanford University Press, 1969), pp. 297–321.

16. Ludwig W. Adamec, "Germany, Third Power in Afghanistan's Foreign Relations," in *Afghanistan: Some New Approaches* (Ann Arbor: The University of Michigan, 1969), p. 245.

17. Ramesh Chandra Ghosh, *Constitutional Documents of the Major Islamic States* (Lahore: Muhammad Ashraf, 1947), p. 128.

18. F. R. Farid, op. cit., p. 16.

19. Surkha, op. cit., p. 92.

20. Hakim Ziai, "Afghanistan's Modernization," *Afghanistan* 16 (July-August-September 1963):41.

21. Ibid., p. 45.

22. Maillart Ella, "Afghanistan's Rebirth: An Interview with H.R.H. Hashim Khan in 1937." *Journal of the Royal Central Asian Society* 27 (April 1940):224.

23. Ibid., p. 227.

24. Hafizullah Emadi, "Afghanistan's Struggle for National Liberation," *Studies in Third World Societies* 27 (March 1984):21–22.

25. Ludwig W. Adamec, "Germany, Third Power in Afghanistan's Foreign Relations," p. 245.

26. "Constitution of Afghanistan 1964," *The Kabul Times Annual 1964* (Kabul: The Kabul Times Publishing Agency, 1964).

27. Ibid.

28. M. G. Aslanov et al., "Ethnography of Afghanistan," in *Afghanistan: Some New Approaches* (Ann Arbor: University of Michigan, 1969), p. 20.

29. Afghanistan, Ministry of Planning, *Afghan Agriculture in Figures, Quas 1357* (Kabul: Government Printing House, December 1978), p. 21.

30. Ibid., p. 21.

31. Ibid., p. 28.

32. Akhgar (Sazmani Mubariza Bara-e-Azadi Tabaqa-e-Kargar or Organization for Liberation of Working Class), *Afghanistan* (Tehran, 1980).

33. Vartan Gregorian, op. cit.

34. Ibid.

35. Louis Dupree, *Afghanistan* (Princeton: Princeton University Press, 1973), p. 439.

36. Hasan Kakar, "Trends in Modern Afghan History," in *Afghanistan in the 1970s* (New York: Praeger Publishers, 1974), p. 22.

37. Marvin Brant, "Recent Economic Development," in *Afghanistan in the 1970s* (New York: Praeger Publishers, 1974), p. 39.

38. Surkha, op. cit.

39. *The Quarterly Economic Review: Pakistan, Afghanistan* (London: The Economist Intelligence Unit, 1967 no. 2), p. 15.

40. Ibid., 1973, no. 2, p. 17.

41. Louis Dupree, "The Emergence of Technocrats in Modern Afghanistan: Changing Patterns of Socio-Political Stratification: 1880–1973," *AUFS Reports* 17 (August 1974):10.

42. *The Quarterly Economic Review of Pakistan and Afghanistan, Annual Supplement* 1985, op. cit., p. 42.

2 Politics of Change and Development

MODERNIZATION IN AFGHANISTAN AFTER WORLD WAR II

Following World War II one of the major goals of the ruling class in Afghanistan was a gradual modernization of the country's socioeconomic structure. The modernization program can be divided into the following categories:

The rise of modern militarism

The birth of political liberalism

Modernization of ideological apparatuses

The politics of land reform

The era of constitutional development

The Rise of Modern Militarism

The main concern of the ruling class was securing the internal stability and legitimacy of the monarchy. To accomplish this the leadership resorted to "iron rule" and arbitrary persecution of opposition forces and initiated the building of a modern, standing armed forces. The leadership encouraged the general population to support the building of a modern army and depicted serving in the army as a service to the Islamic faith and the country. In the beginning approximately 90,000 men enlisted to serve for two years. Army officers, however, were recruited on a permanent basis. The state spent 60 percent of the nation's revenue on building a modern army.[1]

The army was under the full control of the monarch and his family. The king's uncle, Shah Mahmood, was appointed minister of war. The state equipped the army with German, Italian, and British arms. The state opened up political-military training courses and revamped the curriculum of the military academy. Most military departments were reorganized and military manuals and instructions were translated into Persian and Pushtu, the official languages of the country. Military instructors and advisors from Germany, Italy, and Turkey were invited to Afghanistan to train the country's armed forces and military cadets were sent to India, Italy, Japan, and Turkey for further training.

The Ministry of War, under the direction of Shah Mahmood, recruited sons of tribal chiefs for the military academy to train as military officers. Recruitment of the sons of the tribal chiefs from various parts of the country into the armed forces was based on these political considerations: (a) depicting the army as a national institution, and (b) showing that the people are also active participants in the state apparatus.[2] The state also attempted to modernize the gendarmery under the jurisdiction of the Ministry of Interior. Opposition to such a modernization project was severely castigated. Prisons were filled with numerous alleged political prisoners and many of these prisoners died during their imprisonment. Due to mounting opposition Premier Hashim resigned in 1946 and his brother Shah Mahmood was appointed prime minister.

The period that Shah Mahmood served as premier coincided with significant changes in international politics. World War II ended and the United States emerged as a leading world power. India was partitioned and Pakistan was established in 1947. Afghanistan joined the United Nations as a permanent member. Afghanistan's relationship with the Soviet Union had soured since the downfall of King Amanullah in 1929. The leadership in Afghanistan was not pleased with the Soviet Union's support to the resistance forces favoring the restoration of the throne for King Amanullah. King Nadir and his successor King Zahir remained cautious in their relations with the Soviet Union and did not establish any cultural exchange program with it until the mid-1950s, when King Zahir was convinced that such cultural exchange did not threaten political stability in the country.

Afghanistan's relations with Pakistan also remained hostile because of the dispute over the fate of Pushtunistan. The leadership in Afghanistan did not welcome Pakistan's independence and voted against its admission into the United Nations as a permanent member. The period of Shah Mahmood's premiership also coincided with a growing number of intellectuals in Afghanistan. Most of these intellectuals were dismayed with the slow rate of socioeconomic development. The intellectual strata, anxious for progressive changes, began organizing themselves to fight for socioeconomic reforms. This resulted in the formation of the Students Union in 1950 and their subsequent struggle for social and political change in the country.

To maintain stability Premier Shah Mahmood pursued and practiced the "carrot and stick" policy toward opposition forces. Internal repression, soaring prices, and a decline in the people's standard of living generated opposition. It was during this time that

a group of armed men formulated a secret plan to overthrow the monarchy once and for all. The plan was supposed to be carried out on the eve of Afghanistan New Year, March 21, but it was reported to the government by one of its members, and the government detained numerous people in this connection.[3]

To further consolidate the state apparatus Premier Shah Mahmood equipped the army with modern weaponry. The state had sought military aid from the United States in 1944. This and subsequent requests for military assistance were ignored by the U.S. government on the grounds that "the immediate Soviet objective is sufficiently served by the existing isolation and backwardness of the country (Afghanistan)," and since "the Soviet Union has no reason to be dissatisfied with the present situation . . . [it] is unlikely to develop a more active policy in that country under present circumstances."[4] The U.S. government declined another request by the leadership in Afghanistan for military aid on the following grounds:

1. Owing to limitations in manpower and productive potential in the event of war, it is only on the basis of regional cooperation between Afghanistan, Iran, Pakistan and India that Afghanistan would be able to offer more than

a token resistance to invasion from the North. The prospects for cooperation among these four countries at the present time are not promising.

2. The need for allocating our not unlimited resources to the first line of defense, in other words, Western Europe.

3. The present government has maintained its stability for seventeen years. Although the country is faced with problems of inflation and great poverty, the economy is not in a critical condition and there is not yet a grave internal threat to the stability of the government. For these reasons it is considered that assistance beyond a small loan for development purposes and assistance in buying military equipment to assure the Government's ability to maintain internal order is not advisable at this time.[5]

Social opposition to Shah Mahmood's government led to his resignation on 3 September 1953; he was succeeded by his nephew, Mohammad Daoud. Premier Daoud pursued his uncle's domestic policy of suppressing social opposition forces and devoted most of his time to promoting Pushtun nationalism. The external reflection of Pushtun nationalism manifested itself in Afghanistan's policy toward Pakistan over the issue of the Durand Line. (The Durand Line, which was drawn by the British colonial government in 1893, separates the Pushtun and Baluch people between Afghanistan and Pakistan.)

Premier Daoud also requested military assistance from the United States and for this reason he sent his brother Mohammad Naim to Washington on 8 October 1954 to make a personal appeal to John Foster Dulles for U.S. military assistance. Two months after the visit on 28 December 1954 the U.S. government informed the leadership in Afghanistan of its decision to withhold the delivery of military assistance to the country until the latter resolved the "Pushtunistan" dispute with the government of Pakistan. In the meantime the U.S. government extended its military assistance to Pakistan as a result of Pakistan's membership in the U.S.-sponsored South East Asia Treaty Organization (SEATO) and the Baghdad Pact (later CENTO).

The ruling class in Afghanistan perceived U.S. military support to Pakistan as a major threat to political stability in Afghanistan and requested the U.S. government to offer an equivalent amount of military aid to Afghanistan as well, but the U.S. government again declined to provide. such military aid, compelling Premier Daoud to turn to the Soviet Union for such assistance. During an emergency session of the *Loya Jirgah* (Grand Assembly of Tribal Leaders) in March 1955 which included 1,000 representatives from all tribal groups of Afghanistan, a unanimous decision was reached to request the Soviet Union to provide military assistance to Afghanistan. In the meantime the *Loya Jirgah* decided to terminate all U.S. development projects in the country and turn them over to the East European countries.[6]

The U.S. refusal to offer economic and military aid to Afghanistan yet provide military assistance to Pakistan generated anti-U.S. sentiment within a section of the ruling class concentrated around Premier Daoud to the extent that Premier Daoud turned down the U.S. invitation to Afghanistan to join the CENTO Pact. This anti-U.S. sentiment was further aggravated when the government of Pakistan closed its border with Afghanistan in 1961, blocking Afghanistan's trade route and causing a great deal of economic suffering to the country. During this crisis the Soviet Union extended help to Afghanistan and airlifted the country's imported goods from the port of Karachi, Pakistan. The Soviet's timely assistance induced social forces associated with Premier Daoud to further strengthen the country's ties with the Soviet Union.

In December 1955 Soviet leaders visited Afghanistan and promised major economic aid to the country's modernization and development projects. During the visit, leaders of both countries renewed the Afghan-Soviet Neutrality and Non-Aggression Treaty which was concluded between the two countries in 1931 (based on the earlier treaty in 1926). Accordingly, the Soviet Union provided military equipment such as 11 MiG-15 fighters, 1 TL-15 cargo plane, 2 MI-4 helicopters, 24 mobile radio units, and small arms.[7] Prior to the 1978 military coup, the strength of the Afghan army had risen to 100,000 men and the air force to 10,000, with an estimated $600 million of military assistance.[8]

As the result of massive Soviet military assistance to Afghanistan the Ministry of Defense turned to the Soviet Union for training of its military cadres and personnel. According to U.S. documents, 3,725 students and personnel received higher military training in the Soviet Union between 1955 and 1979, and 9,725 Soviet military technicians served in Afghanistan during that period.[9]

Alarmed at the increasingly close ties developing between Afghanistan and the Soviet Union, the U.S. government, in an attempt to regain its influence, revised its policy toward Afghanistan and provided a small amount of military aid and also provided scholarships for a limited number of military officers to study in the United States. Theodore L. Eliot, Jr., former U.S. ambassador to Afghanistan (1973-1978), during a discussion on 2 July 1987 told the author that annually 15 to 20 military officers from Afghanistan were awarded scholarships for higher military training in the U.S. military academies. Approximately 487 military officers received military training in the U.S. from 1958 to 1978.[10]

Due to Soviet military assistance Afghanistan's army was modernized and became instrumental in maintaining stability in the country. This situation and the role of the army as a base of power led many scholars to regard the army in Afghanistan politics as a "state within a state." For instance, during the constitutional period (1963-1973) six governments were formed and fell, but the minister of defense held on throughout. Thus Soviet economic and military assistance to Afghanistan made the latter militarily dependent on the former.

The Birth of Political Liberalism

The socioeconomic policy of profitable commerce that the ruling class in Afghanistan pursued was in sharp contradiction with the interests of numerous members of the middle class and petty bourgeoisie and those intellectuals closely related to them. The growing contradiction among various social strata gave rise to oppositional sentiments which found expression in the founding of several liberal political movements.

The liberal intellectuals' main concern was the political liberalization of various aspects of life in Afghanistan, adoption of a new constitution, and better opportunities for the middle class in politics. The agitation for such liberal ideas that reflected the interests of the middle class culminated in the formation of the political organization of *Wishzalmayan* (the Awakened Youth). Members of the organization did not exceed 100 and came from various social backgrounds (petty bourgeoisie, clerks, intellectuals, and Muslim clerics). The organization was led by Mohammad Rasul, a Pushtun landowner from Kandahar province. The most active members of the organization were Dr. Abdurrauf Benawa, Abdul Hay Habibi, and Gul Pacha Ulfat.

During the initial stage, members of the organization were involved in educational activities and at a latter stage in politics. They ran for seats in the 1949 parliamentary election. Several members of the organization were elected deputies. These intellectuals used the parliament as a tribune to express their liberal ideas and politicize the people; they believed that they could regulate the work of the state apparatus by winning a majority in the parliament. They also advocated freedom of the press so that they could propagate their political ideas. Since the state had already consolidated its base of power and did not see any immediate threat from these social groups, it conceded to some of their demands.

In addition to the Wishzalmayan several other political organizations emerged with quite similar political orientations. The most important among them were Nida-e-Khalq and Watan. The leading ideologist of the Nida-e-Khalq was Dr. Abdurrahman Mahmoodi. Other members were Maulana Khan Mohammad Hasta of Mazari Sharif province; Mohammad Naim Shayan, an official of the Ministry of Finance; engineer Wali Ahmad Ataye; and Mahmoodi's brothers, Lieutenant Mohammad Aman, Mohammad Rahim, a physician, and Mohammad Azim, an official. The organizations published the following periodicals:

1. *Angar* (Burning Embers) by Faiz Mohammad Angar
2. *Nida-e-Khalq* (The Voice of the People) by Dr. Abdurrahman Mahmoodi
3. *Watan* (Homeland) by Mir Ghulam Mohammad Ghubar and Abdul Hay Aziz
4. *Ulus* (People) by Gul Pacha Ulfat.[11]

In an editorial, the Nida-e-Khalq stated that the paper would base itself on the principles of democracy and struggle for the people's rights. It denounced despotism and tyranny and the exploitation of suffering people in Afghanistan and set its task as educating the masses and showing them the way to achieve a government by the people and for the people. The paper strongly denounced the monopoly of economic power by the bureaucratic bourgeoisie and stated that "one of the causes of the people's impoverishment is the fact that money and land are being concentrated in the hands of a limited number of people, that is, becoming their private monopoly."[12]

In 1951, intellectuals who identified with Nida-e-Khalq organized themselves into a political party named *Khalq* (People). The founder of the party was Dr. Mahmoodi. The party was dissolved in 1952 because it could not establish links with the people and its leadership's activities were confined primarily to political agitation among students at Kabul University. Intellectuals associated with the Watan organization advocated social justice and socioeconomic reforms. Members of this organization came from various social backgrounds. The leaders of the organization were Mir Ghulam Mohammad Ghubar and Ahmad Ali Kohzad, both well-known historians, and General Fateh.

Later the ruling class viewed the works and political agitation of these bourgeois-democratic organizations as a threat to political stability. In order to diffuse their influence, intellectuals of upper and middle class backgrounds concentrated around Minister of Defense Mohammad Daoud, King Zahir's cousin, and formed their own party called the *Club-e-Milli* (National Club). The club was financed by Minister of Economics Abdul Majid Zabuli, the richest merchant in Afghanistan.[13]

During the eighth parliamentary elections in 1952 the bourgeois-democratic organizations lost the election. Accusing the government of falsifying the election, they staged a massive demonstration which was joined by students from Kabul University. The state used the army to disperse the demonstrators and the following day imprisoned the leading personalities of the movement. As a result of such repression Abdul Hay Habibi left the country and settled in Pakistan where he issued the Journal *Azad Afghanistan* (Free Afghanistan), which criticized the royal family; Abdurrauf Benawa was deported to India; Mir Ghulam Mohammad Ghubar was sentenced to four years imprisonment, and Dr. Mahmoodi to nine years imprisonment.

Since the National Club did not have a progressive economic development strategy on its political platform to address a broad section of the country's population, it could not appeal to the people and failed to win national patriotic forces to its side. It managed, however, to weaken the position of Premier Shah Mahmood in the government and forced him to resign and give the premiership to Mohammad Daoud in 1953.

The decade of Daoud's premiership (1953-1963) is considered by most scholars in Afghanistan to be a decade of rapid socioeconomic development and modernization. Premier Daoud, considered the Prince Sihanouk of Afghanistan by upper and middle class intellectuals, embarked upon various state-sponsored modernization projects. One of his major projects concerned the freedom of women. In 1959 the wives of the royal family and top government officials led a movement to end the use of the veil.[14] Scholars of development schools attribute women's emancipation to Daoud's leadership but often forget the role of external capital in the modernization process in Afghanistan.

[T]he influx of foreign commodities (luxury items) flooded internal markets in Afghanistan and the merchant bourgeoisie needed consumers for these commodities. . . . Therefore, women's emancipation, in addition to many other factors, was considered a historical necessity of the time.[15]

Although conservative social strata, clerics, and tribal chiefs in several provinces denounced state policies concerning the unveiling of women, intellectuals of upper and middle classes supported it on the grounds that it was a step forward toward women's freedom. Premier Daoud was encouraged by these intellectuals to carry out his policies of women's freedom in the countryside. During a visit to Kandahar, Premier Daoud encouraged the wives of government employees to discard their veils. This provoked conservative clerics and tribal leaders to stage a massive protest demonstration. Premier Daoud used the military to crush the opposition to his "women's movement" and to teach a lesson to opposition forces elsewhere. Tanks and aircraft fighters raided villages for several days. As a result more than 600 people, including religious and tribal leaders, were arrested and executed in the capital penitentiaries. During Daoud's premiership no political parties were permitted to engage in political activities and no private presses were allowed publication. The state virtually controlled the press and all forms of mass communications. Foreign journals were thoroughly censored and many were banned from the country.

Opposition to Premier Daoud's policies of social and economic development gradually began within and without the state apparatus. Western-educated elites of the upper and middle classes concentrated around King Zahir regarded Premier Daoud's close ties with the Soviet Union a danger to Afghanistan's "independence." As their numbers increased, the intelligentsia chafed against the oppressive character of the state. As the growing dissatisfaction among the people became more widespread, some members of King Zahir's family began to agitate for a liberalization of government policy. They feared a revolt could be possible if things did not change, and saw as a solution the removal of Premier Daoud from power and the return to a government elected by parliament. Those in the leadership position concentrated around Premier Daoud advocated a status quo, and did not take the possibility of a revolution seriously. This contradiction within the leadership circle resulted in a two-way struggle that would eventually decide Premier Daoud's fate.

King Zahir began active participation in the government, and used his title and influence to rally popular support. He toured provinces, reviewed military units, all with the goal of establishing himself among the people and military and gaining public loyalty. King Zahir's uncle, Shah Wali, the top military officer used his own reputation and popularity to sway the loyalties of the country's military commanders away from Premier Daoud. Abdul Wali, King Zahir's son-in-law, also used his position in the military establishment to rally support and to facilitate behind-the-scenes maneuvering which gave the king increased bargaining power aimed at making changes in the current leadership. Through the efforts of these three men and their supporters, a dominant group emerged with King Zahir at its head, and Premier Daoud's resignation was now only a matter of time.[16]

As the result of such a struggle within the ruling class Premier Daoud resigned and King Zahir appointed Dr. Mohammad Yusuf prime minister on 9 March 1963. King Zahir also appointed a seven-man committee to draft a new constitution. The final draft, which was endorsed in 1964, was based on Western constitutional models and incorporated elements of the Islamic faith and local traditions. During the constitutional period (1963-1973) Western-educated elites were in the upper echelon of the administration, governing the country's socioeconomic policy.

Modernization of Ideological Apparatuses

The modernization of ideological apparatuses (schools, the means of mass communication, etc.) began as early as the 1920s during the reign of King Amanullah. But rapid modernization and improvement of educational systems didn't occur until after World War II, when the country increased contacts with international communities. Secular education was being stressed and religious influences that dominated educational systems for centuries began to decline.

Following World War II several Western countries such as Britain, France, Germany, and the United States provided technical assistance to Afghanistan. English was taught in high schools (from the sophomore to senior year) throughout the country. Several high schools in Kabul were patterned on the Western model. French was the medium of instruction in Estiqlal, German in Nijat, and English in Habibiya and Ghazi high schools until the 1960s when stirrings of nationalism began to occur, and use of foreign language as the medium of instruction was replaced by that of the vernacular, Dari (Persian) and Pushtu.

Since the mid-1950s, U.S. influence has asserted itself mostly in the organization and curricula of village and vocational schools, and in teachers' training. But its active participation in modernizing the country's educational system began in the early 1960s when "the United States was urged by the Prime Minister, and has now agreed to contribute 60 percent of the expenditures, in Dollars and Afghanis, toward building 35 primary schools and 120 Middle-Grade classrooms in Kabul."[17] The United States Agency for International Development (USAID) provided $4 million for the construction of the Afghan Institute of Technology (AIT) in 1951 and provided AIT with teachers, advisors, and laboratory equipments.[18]

In 1964, the United States extended economic assistance to modernize and enlarge Kabul University. All colleges which were previously dispersed in various sections of Kabul were consolidated on a new campus with USAID assistance. Classrooms, administrative buildings, laboratories, and a dormitory were added. The cost totalled Afs. 324,176,811 which included $7,156,221 paid by USAID.[19] Kabul University also received substantial aid from the University of Wyoming and Columbia University. "The College of Engineering was established with USAID aid. The five-year program and administration of the faculty follow essentially an American model. Most of the faculty have received graduate training in the United States."[20] The United States also provided scholarships for students and scholars to study in U.S. universities and about 105 American personnel served in Afghanistan, excluding Peace Corps and other volunteer groups.[21] The number of scholars and students that were offered grants by various U.S. agencies reached 2,401 since 1958.[22] The number of students who came at their own expense or through other international agencies is not available, but it does not exceed 2,000.

The United States also participated in modernizing Afghanistan's communication media and film industry and provided training opportunities for people with journalism backgrounds and other related fields.[23] The news agencies of the United Press International (UPI) and the Associated Press (AP) supplied news and documentaries to Afghanistan media.[24] The United States Information Service (USIS) provided film and documentaries for the country's intellectual strata in English and offered English courses.[25]

The Soviet Union in contention with the United States for influence in Afghanistan also participated in the country's modernization projects since 1965, providing financial aid to modernize educational institutions, financing the building of several vocational schools in Kabul, and organizing training courses for technical personnel. One of the major

Soviet contributions in modernizing Afghanistan's educational institutions was the building of Kabul Polytechnic Institute, begun in 1964 with a loan of $6.2 million. The Institute was completed in 1966 with five main departments covering 18 major fields with an emphasis on architecture and civil, electrical, and mechanical engineering. According to the Afghanistan-U.S.S.R. agreement 17 Soviet professors were hired to administer and teach at the institute.[26] Approximately 1,050 Soviet personnel served Afghanistan between 1955 and 1971.[27]

The Soviet Union also provided scholarships for students for higher studies in the U.S.S.R. The total number of students who studied in the Soviet Union is estimated to be 4,000 between 1955 and 1979.[28] On the basis of official data available it is estimated that 70,000 skilled workers had been trained in the U.S.S.R. between 1955 and 1985.[29] The Soviet Union also provided news and cultural documentaries for local consumption. The Soviet embassy in Kabul distributes illustrated pamphlets dealing with economic, scientific, and educational progress in the Soviet Union. The Soviet News Agency *Telegrafone Agentsvo Sovietskogo Soyuza* (TASS) supplied news to Afghan news agencies.[30]

Among the students who studied in the United States, approximately one-third of them did not return to Afghanistan or later emigrated to the U.S. after initially taking up positions in the country.[31] The reason they gave was marriage or health problems but a few cited political asylum. Another reason might be that most students were attracted by lucrative employment opportunities in U.S. companies. Thus many remained in the United States and failed to play an active role in the process of sociopolitical and economic transformation in Afghanistan.

On the other hand, all of the Afghan students who completed their higher studies in the U.S.S.R. returned home and worked in Afghanistan even though a few were married to Russians. Most of these groups of intellectuals were associated with the army and would not have been allowed to leave their jobs to go elsewhere. In addition to this most army officers were imbued with Soviet-style Marxism and upon their return home a number of these people had established links with the pro-Soviet People's Democratic Party of Afghanistan (PDPA) and actively worked toward a political change in the country.

The Politics of Land Reform

Most of Afghanistan's population are landless peasants and farmers. The deteriorating living conditions of the peasantry, on the one hand,

and feudal oppression on the other were forcing the landless peasants to fight for better living conditions. Following World War II the continuous peasant uprisings were forcing the leadership in Afghanistan to find ways to improve the situation to prevent the further escalation of such uprisings. The peasant situation was so badly deteriorating that even the country's semi-official paper *Islah* began to write about the plight of the peasants back in the late 1940s and call for agrarian reform. "Land reform" initiated by the state was designed, on the one hand, to deflect future peasant uprisings by bringing arable land under cultivation and distributing it among the landless peasants and, on the other hand, to bring some sectors of the agricultural project under the sway of capitalism. In this way the leadership was trying to disarm the revolutionary intentions of the peasant population.

To silence the cry of the peasantry, the leadership in Afghanistan, with the help of the United States, initiated major programs of development that would provide land for landless peasants in the Hilmand Valley in the southern part of the country. The U.S.-based Morrison-Knudsen Company (MKC) undertook the construction of the project in late 1945. MKC finished a 145-foot-high dam which is 1,740 feet long and has a storage capacity of 157,085.02 hectare-feet of water in 1952.[32] The site chosen for the first farming experiment was the Nadi Ali district located ten miles from the locally known "New York of Afghanistan," Lashkargah, the center of Hilmand province. The prime objective of the state, by settling the Pushtun nomads and other landless peasants of Paktiya province into that region was to use these new settlers as a death squad to crush the uprisings of the non-Pushtun people of the west, southwest, and central part of the country. It was hoped that the peasants would control and supervise the movements of the nomads and landless peasants of Paktiya province who usually traveled back and forth in the mountainous areas. Previously it had been difficult for the state to control and maintain its authority over the nomads.

When the project was completed, the state managed to settle 3,000 families (mainly Pushtuns) and about 1,200 nomads in Nadi Ali district by giving each family a piece of land. According to the state plan, the settlers were supposed to pay the balance of 16,800 Afghanis or $320 ($1.00 is equal to 50 Afghanis) over a 20-year period. Once they paid the full debt to the state, then the title to the land would be given to them.[33]

However, problems began to arise soon after the people were settled in the Hilmand Valley. Improper land survey was likely a contributing factor in the failure to discover that there was a substratum of impenetrable boulder conglomerates only a few inches below the soil surface. Plowed topsoil tended to be washed away quickly or became saturated with salts. The families found that their allotted plots were too small to adequately support them, and their houses were located at an inconvenient distance from the fields, sometimes as much as four kilometers. Eventually problems related to ethnocentrism developed, and the project finally collapsed when the people began to leave the area.[34]

When the project collapsed, the state transferred these people and many other landless Pushtun peasants to the northern part of the country among other nationalities such as Uzbek, Turkman, and Tadjiks. It is due to this reason that today Pushtun tribes are widely scattered throughout the country, especially in western and northern areas of the country where the indigenous people do not have any historical ties with the Pushtun tribes.[35] The arbitrary settlement of Pushtuns in other areas of the country was carried out through displacement of the indigenous population and appropriation of their landed properties. Following the implementation of this policy a bloody confrontation took place between immigrants and the indigenous populace. This policy made Pushtun tribes a threat to the non-Pushtun tribes of the country.

The economic development and the transfer of prospective landless Pushtun tribes among other nationalities to the north did not lessen social tensions, but further stimulated the traditionally suspicious peasants (both new and old villagers) to resist and continue to fight feudal oppression. The peasant uprisings in rural areas were threatening the ruling class every day because their revolutionary potential had been seen before: in the enormous uprisings of 1891 in Hazarajat; 1896 in Nuristan; 1912-13 in Paktiya and Kandahar; 1968 in Kabul (Paghman), Parwan, Maimana, Nimroz, Farah, and Badghis; and the 1971 uprising in Ghor province,[36] and their participation in any democratic revolution was essential. These circumstances forced the leadership to find other alternatives so as to be able to bring future peasant uprisings under control and to prevent their alignment with other revolutionary movements in the country.

A section of the bureaucratic bourgeoisie who benefited from trade with the Soviet Union and the Soviet-educated intellectuals within the state apparatus, and who were dismayed with political and economic developments in Afghanistan opted for large-scale estatism (state-guided economic development) as an alternative development strategy and requested the Soviet Union to extend economic and technical assistance. The Soviet Union loaned Afghanistan $3.5 million[37] to assist the country's development projects and to alleviate the agrarian problem in the country. The Soviets participated in organizing two big citrus fruit farms with a total area of 5,000 hectares in the Jalal Abad Valley. These farms—Hadda and Ghaziabad—were the country's first mechanized agricultural enterprises built by the Soviet Union and more than 9,000 persons, formerly landless peasants, are now working on these two state farms.[38]

Although this economic development strategy led to a semi-modernization of agriculture in some parts of the country, it also resulted in commercialization of agriculture and contributed to the rapid proletarianization of the peasantry and the concentration of land both to the state and the landed propertied classes. The dispossessed farmers and peasants had to work as sharecroppers or increasingly as wage laborers. Furthermore, these agricultural projects not only tied the country's economy to that of the Soviet Union but also provided a market for Soviet commodities such as chemical fertilizers, Soviet-made Byelarus tractors, etc.[39] Thus Afghanistan's economic dependence on the Soviet Union resulted in the country's being compelled to buy Soviet manufactured goods, to employ hundreds of Soviet technicians and even skilled workers in Soviet-sponsored state development projects, and to export locally produced goods to the Soviet Union.

The Decade of Constitutional Development

The period of 1963-1973 is considered to be a decade of experimental democracy in Afghanistan. A new constitution was drafted in 1963 and was endorsed a year later. The constitution legalized the existence of politial parties, granted freedom of speech and of assembly, and allowed publication of private papers, subject to state censorship after publication. Following the endorsement of the constitution several political parties, espousing various political ideologies, emerged. They are: (1) *Hizbi Demokratiki Khalqi Afghanistan* (The People's Democratic Party of Afghanistan or PDPA); (2) *Sazmani Demokratiki Navin-e-Afghanistan* (The New Democratic Organization of Afghanistan) known as *Shula-e-Jawid* (Eternal Flame); (3) *Afghan Millat* (Social Democratic

Party); and (4) *Sazmani Jawanani Musulman* known as Eikhwan-ul-Muslimin or the "Islamic Brotherhood."

The People's Democratic Party of Afghanistan (PDPA) supported the constitution and participated in parliamentary elections. The party did not support a social revolution from the bottom but it concentrated its work among army officers within the armed forces with the hope of making a "revolution" possible from above. The PDPA supported the political and ideological position of the Communist Party of the Soviet Union in the national and international arena. The PDPA split into two factions: *Khalq* (the People) and *Parcham* (the Flag) because of political differences as well as the cult of personality which developed within their leaderships. Although both parties supported the monarchy, the *Parchamis* were known more for their collaboration with state and the royal court. During a speech in Parliament Babrak Karmal said:

It is the duty of each and every Afghan subject to pay his heartfelt respect to such a King who, I dare to say, is considered the most progressive of all the Kings in the monarchist countries of Asia. This is the right which we sincerely believe in and revere, and no one can deprive us of this right to respect such a progressive king. . . . It should be well to entrust the honorable Assembly, in contact with the Ministry of Finance, to render new Terms of the Royal Court, so that the authority and prestige of our King will be established and preserved.[40]

Since the Social Democratic Party, Afghan Millat, agitated Pushtun nationalism and the Islamic Brotherhood, Sazmani Jawanani Musulman, that of Islamicization of the state apparatus, they did not pose an immediate threat to the status quo in Afghanistan. The government did not take their activities seriously as compared to that of the New Democratic Organization (*Shula-e-Jawid*) which defied participation in the parliament and articulated a revolutionary overthrow of the state.

In 1965 King Zahir asked Premier Mohammad Yusuf, who headed the interim government (1963-1965), to continue his job as prime minister. On this basis Premier Yusuf selected a cabinet and went to the *Wolusi Jirgah* (House of the People) to secure a vote of confidence. Premier Yusuf designated several veteran bureaucrats to serve in his cabinet. This generated antagonism and opposition in the Parliament and Premier Yusuf failed to secure the needed vote of confidence. The monarchists, backed by military force, pressured the Parliament to reconsider the matter. As a result, on 25 October 1965, in a closed session the Parliament cast its vote for Yusuf's government. Most people, particularly the intellectuals who wanted a change in the government, marched in protest on the Parliament. The government security forces encountered the demonstrators in the vicinity of the Parliament and the outcome was a bloody confrontation between the two. As a result 40 people were killed and numerous others were wounded.[41] Students now annually celebrate the day of the shootings, *Seumi Akrab* (October 25), as the beginning of the era of a new democratic movement in Afghanistan. Following this incident Premier Yusuf resigned and on 4 November 1965 King Zahir appointed Mohammad Hashim Maiwandwal, minister of information and culture and former Afghanistan ambassador to the United States, as the new prime minister.

In order to appease students and intellectuals, Premier Maiwandwal participated at a memorial meeting that Kabul University students held for their compatriots who died during the October twenty-fifth demonstration and promised to investigate and punish responsible authorities. But the promise remained unfulfilled. To reduce the influence of the opposition political parties, Premier Maiwandwal established his own party, the Progressive Democratic Party known as *Musawati* (Equalitarian), and used his influence to enlist state officials into the party. In April 1967 Premier Maiwandwal was accused of being a CIA front in an article in *Ramparts*, "How the U.S. Turns Foreign Students into Traitors," written by the editor interviewing Afghan student Abdul Latif Hotaki. As a result Maiwandwal resigned in November 1967 stating poor health as the reason for his resignation. Maiwandwal went to the United States for medical treatment and was hospitalized in the U.S. Air Force Hospital at Andrews Air Force Base outside Washington.[42]

Mr. Noor Ahmad Etemadi succeeded Premier Maiwandwal and remained in office from October 1967 to October 1969. Etemadi's government failed to solve the pressing socioeconomic problems. His tenure as premier coincided with student and worker unrest throughout the country. Soaring prices and the deteriorating living conditions of the people resulted in worker demonstrations and strikes (see Table 2.1) which were mainly supported and led by members of the New Democratic Organization (*Shula-e-Jawid*). Since there were no trade unions or labor unions to defend the rights of the workers and represent their demand for higher economic and social compensation, the demonstrations and strikes were the only means that the workers could use to express their grievances.

The New Democratic Organization concentrated its political and

Table 2.1
Chronology of Workers' Strikes, 1968

Month	Strike	Location
April	Workers of Kuhsar Textile Co.	Kabul
May	Workers of Jangalak Plant	Kabul
	Workers of Government Printing Press	Kabul
	Government Bus and Lorry Drivers	Kabul
	Workers of Puli Charkhi Textile and Bicycle Assembly Plants	Kabul
	Workers of Kandahar Woolen Mill	Kandahar
	Workers of Ghori Cement Plant	Baghlan
	Workers of Puli Khumri Textile Co.	Baghlan
	Workers of Petroleum Industry in Shiberghan (March towards Kabul turned back at Salang pass)	Jowzjan
	Workers of asphalting unit of Puli Khumri-Shiberghan road project	Samangan

June	Workers of Spirzar Cotton Co.	Kunduz
	Workers of Education Press	Kabul
	Workers of Gulbahar Textile Co.	Parwan
	Workers at Jabul Seraj	Parwan
	Workers of Ghori Cement Plant (second strike)	Baghlan
	Goldminers of Norabeh	Takhar
	Workers of Hajari-Nadjari Plant	Kabul
	Workers of Puli Khumri Textile Co. (second strike)	Baghlan
	Workers of Kandahar Fruit Co. (thirty-five workers laid off)	Kandahar
	Workers of Hazrati Imam and Spirzar Cotton Co. Peasants joined port workers at Bandar-e-Sher Khan on 6 June	Kunduz
	Strike of Jangalak workers explodes into violence	Kabul

Sources: General Union of Democratic and Patriotic Afghans (GUDSPA), *Independent Afghanistan* 18 (March-April 1983):11. Louis Dupree, *Afghanistan* (Princeton: Princeton University Press, 1973).

Table 2.2
Chronology of Students' Strikes, 1968

Month	Strike	Location
April	Students strike	Nimroz
May	2,000 high school students who had failed Kabul University's entrance examinations	Kabul
	Students at Afghan Institute of Technology, Technicum, School of Nursing, Teacher's Training College (two students killed)	Kabul
	Students at Kabul University, Faculties of Theology, Law and Medicine for graduate programs	Kabul

June	Students at Teacher's Training School in solidarity with Kunduz workers strike	Kunduz
	Students in support of workers strike in Gulbahar	Parwan
	Students in support of workers strike in Jabul Seraj	Parwan
	Students at Paktiya Teacher's Training School and High School	Paktiya
	Students strike at Afghan Institute of Technology continues	Kabul
	Students at Kabul University (Faculty of Education)	Kabul
	Students strike of Faculties of Law and Medicine continues	Kabul
	Students joined workers and peasants protest demonstration	Kunduz

Sources: General Union of Democratic Students and Patriotic Afghans (GUDSPA), *Independent Afghanistan* 18 (March-April 1983):11; Louis Dupree, *Afghanistan* (Princeton: Princeton University Press, 1973).

organizational work among the blue-collar workers and supported their demands for better living conditions, higher wages, insurance, reduction in the working hours, etc. Members and supporters of the organization also celebrated the first day of May as International Working Class Day by organizing rallies in Kabul and other cities. The Islamic organizations neither participated in any such meetings and rallies nor did they support the struggle of the blue-collar workers. Although the Islamic organizations held meetings and rallies, the prime objective of their rallies was to return to an Islamic way of life and the "Islamicization" of the state apparatus. They demanded a ban on alcoholic beverages (even to foreigners), a compulsory restoration of Islamic dress for women (veil), and abolishing of secular education for the female population.

Student movements intensified in the mid-1960s. Students went on strike to protest the bureaucratic procedures and regulations in educational institutions such as the grading system, college admission procedures, etc. They also lent their support to the working class movement. The objective of the most radical section of students associated with the New Democratic Organization was to integrate student movement with that of the working class in the hope of building a mass movement for a new democratic revolution. Table 2.2 shows the peak of students' strikes during the months of May and June 1968.

As a result of the student strikes Kabul University and most colleges in Kabul remained closed. Student strikes in provinces also motivated people to fight social oppression. For instance, in Nangarhar Province, near the border of Pakistan, the Sipai, Mandozai, and Shinwari people launched a major assault on state agencies and seized a gendarmery outpost and gathered all available weapons. In Jalal Abad demonstrators occupied the state-owned Spinzar Hotel and attacked various other government agencies.[43] Although the government struck hard on the demonstrators and maintained stability, social unrest continued throughout the country. The growing social opposition and pressing economic issues forced Prime Minister Etemadi to resign in 1971. Dr. Abdul Zahir, who served twice as speaker of the House of the People, was appointed prime minister.

The designated prime minister had intended to solve the country's pressing issues that his predecessor could not. Unfortunately, time was not on his side. When Premier Zahir assumed office a severe drought struck and famine prevailed throughout the country. As a result tens of thousands of people died of hunger, cold, and malnutrition. Kabul University, which remained closed for 160 days, was reopened as Premier Zahir conceded to some of the students' demands regarding educational policies in Afghanistan's universities. Premier Zahir's policy of appeasing the students resulted in the resignation of the entire body of the senate of Kabul University and the minister of education. This, plus the tension between Premier Zahir's government and Parliament (*Wolusi Jirgah*), resulted in Premier Zahir's resignation in December 1972.

King Zahir appointed Mohammad Musa Shafiq, former minister of foreign affairs, as the new prime minister. In order to maintain political stability Premier Shafiq intended to enforce a law to ban demonstrations and public meetings, close down the free press, and allow publication only of those papers that supported the system. Premier Shafiq resorted to Islam and Islamic ideology in order to expand the social base of his government. For the same reason he extended his tacit support to the *Sazmani Jawanani Musulman* known as the "Islamic Brotherhood."

In foreign policy issues, Premier Shafiq maintained a friendly relationship with the neighboring countries of Iran and Pakistan. On 12 March 1973, Premier Shafiq signed a treaty with the government of Iran which regulated the amount of water to flow from the Hilmand River to Iran. Premier Shafiq also tried to negotiate with the government of Pakistan over the question of the right to self-determinination of Pushtuns residing on the other side of the Durand Line. So that the Soviet Union would not misinterpret the country's foreign policy, Premier Shafiq invited Nikolai Podgorny, then the president of the Supreme Soviet of the USSR, to Afghanistan to assure the Soviet leadership that Afghanistan had no ill intentions toward the Soviet Union in normalizing its relations with the two Western allies, Pakistan and Iran.

During the period of constitutional experience (1963-1973) and Shafiq's premiership, the country's economy went bankrupt and the living conditions of the working class became so miserable that almost one million and a half blue-collar workers emigrated to Iran, Saudi Arabia, and many other Middle Eastern countries.[44] This internal situation was maturing into a grassroots-based social revolution. Various political parties were preparing themselves to seize political power. Shafiq's few months rule as premier ended when former Prime Minister Mohammad

Daoud (1953–1963) staged a military coup in July 1973 and ended the decade of constitutional development in Afghanistan.

THE SUPERPOWERS POLICY OF ECONOMIC ASSISTANCE TO AFGHANISTAN

Afghanistan, owing to lack of skilled manpower and financial resources, could not modernize its backward economic infrastructure. To do so, the ruling class believed it necessary to engage major capitalist countries to assist Afghanistan's modernization projects. The leadership in Afghanistan, viewing the United States as a great power, tried to encourage its leadership to participate in her economic development projects.

In 1934 the U.S. government extended diplomatic recognition to Afghanistan and a year later established an embassy in Kabul. Afghanistan's strategic location (its proximity to the Soviet Union) was of immense significance to the United States. George McGee, while testifying before the U.S. Congress, stated that "Afghanistan is an important country of South Asia and its strategic location further augments its significance."[45] For this reason the United States participated in the country's development programs. U.S. private entrepreneurs visited Afghanistan to study the prospects for capital investment in the country. A U.S. oil company, Inland Exploration Company, conducted research in Afghanistan to examine oil deposits and the possibility of its extraction. The company later abandoned its research on the grounds that it was not economically feasible to extract the country's oil for U.S. markets.

In 1945 the United States signed a contract to loan $20 million to Afghanistan for construction of the Kandahar-Herat highway, the Arghandab and Kajaki water reservoirs, and for completing the Hilmand project. The loan had to be paid back in 18 years and the equipment for the project had to be purchased from the United States. U.S. companies loaned Afghanistan an amount of money equal to what the country had in the U.S. banks, earned from the export of its Karakul skins ($20 million).[46]

A second U.S. loan for these projects was given in 1954 at 4.5 percent interest for a period of 13 years. The U.S. government and U.S. private enterprises invested $51.75 million at an interest rate of four percent from 1946 to 1957. Only eight percent of these loans was spent on the Hilmand project. Due to the bad quality of the soil in the region the project did not yield favorable results.[47]

In March 1946 the U.S. Morrison-Knudsen Company (MKC) signed a contract with the government of Afghanistan for the construction of roads and irrigation systems.[48] According to the contract the project was supposed to be completed in three years. The company loaned $20 million to Afghanistan. But this money was spent on preliminary study of the project in the first two years of the signed contract without achieving any positive results. The MKC made it clear that it had made a mistake in its calculations and the cost of completing the project would require $100 million. The leadership in Afghanistan was forced to borrow more money from the company for completing this project.[49]

The Middle East Journal writes that from 1946 onward the salaries of advisors and technicians of the MKC and the company's expenditures were absorbing the total income from Afghanistan's annual exports to foreign countries.[50] In 1948 the government borrowed $21 million at 4.5 percent interest from the U.S. Export-Import Bank to renew its contract with the MKC. In 1950, the Afghanistan Council of Ministers agreed to renew its contract with the MKC and even expanded the company's sphere of activities in other development projects.[51]

After World War II the United States further expanded its spheres of activities in Afghanistan in order to stem the increasing influence of the Soviet Union in the country as well as the spread of communism in South Asia. According to the U.S. administration,

the U.S. policy toward South Asia is based on, a) the orientation of South Asia toward the United States and other Western democracies and away from the U.S.S.R. [and] b) an endeavor by the United States to meet the legitimate requirements for spare parts and replacements for military equipment of United States origin already possessed by South Asian countries to assist those countries in the maintenance of internal security and freedom from communist domination.[52]

The United States in pursuance of its policy objectives supported the liberal social strata within the ruling class in Afghanistan whom the U.S. administration considered to be an effective agent in serving U.S. interests in the country. According to the U.S. administration, "economic and political progress in Afghanistan is hampered by a conservative, often reactionary, ruling group and we should, therefore, encourage the growing influence of educated liberal Afghans."[53] The U.S. companies also showed great interest in expanding trade relations with Afghanistan. A U.S. trade mission visited the country to examine the prospect of U.S. markets there. The mission concluded that

American manufacturers and exporters must give more attention to the Afghan market. Many products such as automobile and truck tires, trucks and buses, agricultural machinery, commercial ice-making machinery, tannery equipment and shoe-making and construction machinery and materials, appear to us to have an excellent market potential there.[54]

The U.S. loan to Afghanistan prior to the first Five-Year Plan was $91.5 million, while it loaned $97.3 million during the first Five-Year Plan (1957-1961), $155.7 million during the second Five-Year Plan (1963-1967), and $53.1 million during the third Five-Year Plan (1968-1972) to Afghanistan.[55]

A section of the ruling class within the state apparatus concentrated around Premier Mohammad Daoud was dissatisfied with U.S. policies and its development projects and turned to the Soviets for economic assistance in modernizing Afghanistan. The Soviet Union, as a rising power in the 1960s, began to compete with the United States in expanding its spheres of influence. Louis Dupree, an American anthropologist, writes that in November 1959 a Soviet oil exploration team told him "we are here for a long time. The Afghans need our help . . . why don't you Americans go home? Afghanistan is our neighbor not yours."[56]

The political difference between the ruling class in Afghanistan and Pakistan over the issue of Pushtunistan and the Soviet support of Afghanistan's policy made the leadership in Afghanistan look upon the Soviet Union as an alternate source of political, economic, and military support. The Soviet Union, which was looking for just such an opportunity, extended political, economic, and military support to Afghanistan for its own interests in the region. Soviet leader N. S. Khrushchev during his visit to Kabul articulated his country's policy toward Afghanistan as follows:

I went there [to Afghanistan] with Bulganin on our way back from India [in 1955]. It was clear that America was courting Afghanistan. . . . The Americans were undertaking all kinds of projects at their own expenses. . . . The Americans ᶫ ⁻rdly bother to put a fig leaf over their self-centered, militaristic motives. . . .

It's my strong feeling that the capital which we have invested in Afghanistan hasn't been wasted. We have earned the Afghan's trust and friendship, and it hasn't fallen into American trap; it hasn't been caught on the hook baited with American money.[57]

The Soviet leader also expressed his country's support to Afghanistan regarding the dispute between Afghanistan and Pakistan over the issue of Pushtunistan as follows:

We sympathize with Afghanistan's policy on the question of Pushtunistan. The Soviet Union stands for an equitable solution of this problem which cannot be settled correctly without taking into account the vital interests of the peoples inhabiting Pushtunistan.[58]

It is due to this that the Soviet Union increased its export of capital to the country and allied itself with a section of the ruling class within the state apparatus which was in favor of trade with them. Many merchants benefited from trade with the Soviet Union. Merchants from Herat province, for example, including Abdul Majid Zabuli, made substantial profits from trade with the Soviets. Another merchant, Abdul Aziz Londoni, a pioneer in trade with the Soviet Union, developed a cotton production industry in the northern part of Afghanistan solely for Soviet consumption.[59]

The two superpowers extended economic assistance to Afghanistan and subsequently increased their participation in the country's development projects with the hope of winning Afghanistan to their side. To this end the two superpowers tried to improve and develop the country's transportation networks. The Soviets built highways connecting Kabul to the Soviet Union's southern borders. "The construction cost of the road which passes through Puli Khumri, Baghlan and Kunduz and terminates at the Amu River port through which much of Afghanistan-Soviet trade is channeled totalled $12,114,220. The foreign currency expenditure came from a Soviet credit."[60]

Similarly the U.S.-built Kabul-Jalal Abad and Kabul-Kandahar highways connected Kabul to Pakistan borders of Peshawar and Quetta. The United States also provided $7.49 million for building the Herat-Islam Qala road connecting Herat with Iran.[61] The highways made it possible for merchants to import foreign commodities and to export raw materials to the world market.

In the first and second Five-Year Plans efforts were made to improving those raw materials that the capital lenders needed but none for meeting the needs of the people. For example, no priority was given to wheat, which constituted the main staple food of the people. Instead, priority was given to the planting of cotton in the northern part of the country. In Mazari Sharif province,

> there is an area of 280,364.37 hectares that has been under cotton cultivation. It should be mentioned that this new development has decreased by 1/5 the total wheat production per year. Similarly in Maimana province cotton farms cover an area of 281,781.37 hectares. The total cotton cultivation areas in the northern provinces could be 9150 sq. km. . . . The Ministry of Agriculture has imported and introduced a special kind of cotton from the Soviet Union. . . . This new seed has been put under cultivation on experimental farms in Herat province. . . . The most popular customer of Afghanistan cotton is the Soviet Union. The average annual cotton export from Afghanistan is nearly 17,707 tons.[62]

In the first Five-Year Plan, cotton production was raised by 127 percent and sugar beets by 17 percent. During the third Five-Year Plan, the quantity of cotton production was raised by 13 percent and sugar beets by 57 percent.[63] Contrary to this development, agricultural production (to meet the basic needs of the people) declined year after year. For example, wheat production declined from 2,282,000 tons in 1965-66 to 2,033,000 tons in 1966-67 and to 2,000,000 in 1967-68.[64]

The Soviet Union provided $5.6 million prior to the first Five-Year plan, $126.9 million during the first Five-Year Plan, $258.3 million during the second Five-Year Plan, and $126.3 million during the third Five-Year Plan to Afghanistan (see Table 2.3).[65] In the agricultural sector, Soviet aid to Afghanistan was given to those branches that served the interests of the Soviet Union. Since Afghanistan's climate is favorable for many varieties of fruit trees and plants, fruit exports are 25 to 30 percent of total exports. Common fruits are apricot, peach, palm, almond, mulberry, apple, pear, pomegranate, and date. Fruits of the Mediterranean climate such as lemon, orange, and date are only planted in Nangarhar province. The olive tree, which is usually planted in Mediterranean areas, can be found widely in Afghanistan especially in eastern and southeastern provinces.[66]

The Soviet Techno-Export Company engaged in extensive mineral and oil exploration in Afghanistan and conducted a survey of coal and iron deposits as well as gold and lapis lazuli in 1963,[67] and finally took over the country's hydrocarbon industry for themselves. John F. Shroder, an American geologist writes:

Table 2.3
U.S. and USSR Loan and Economic Assistance, 1949–1972 (in millions of dollars)

Country	Aid	Prior to 1st 5-Y Plan	1st 5-Y Plan 1957—1961	2nd 5-Y plan 1963—1967	3rd 5-Y Plan 1968—1972	Total
				Year		
USA	Economic	91.5	97.3	155.7	53.1	397.6
	Military	——	1.2	4.7	——	5.9
USSR	Economic	5.6	126.9	258.3	126.1	516.9
	Military	100.0	NA	NA	NA	100.0

Sources: U.S. Overseas Loans and Grants and Assistance from International Organizations: Obligation and Loan Authorizations, 1 July 1945 - 30 September 1985. p. 8; U.S. United States Embassy, Kabul, *Helping People: U.S. Agency for International Development Mission to Afghanistan April 1979*, p. 35. Afghanistan, Ministry of Planning, *Majmuaei Aisayawi-e-Sali 1350* [Statistical dictionary of 1971] (Kabul: Matbaa-e-Dawlati, 1350 [1971]), p. 161.

The extensive Soviet exploration resulted in additional first-rate geologic reports and maps and identification of over 1,400 mineral showings or concurrence as well as 70-odd commercial deposits. The Soviets then committed over $652 million in oil for further resource exploration and development, including a half-million-ton oil refinery, a 1.5 million tons per year copper smelter, and many other projects. . . . Afghan cement manufactured at world quality is now reportedly sent to the U.S.S.R. for export to the world market and replaced in Afghanistan with low-standard Soviet cement.[68]

When the Soviet Union began to engage in extensive exploration of Afghanistan's mineral and oil resources many Western technical advisors from both the Ministry of Mines and Industries and from the Cartographic Institute were removed.[69] In the late 1960s a Soviet-Afghanistan technical contract for the extraction of natural gas was signed between the two countries. According to this contract the gas had to be exported to the Soviet Union for ten years and the Soviet Union agreed to "pay $0.174 and $0.19 per 1,000 c.f. of gas to Afghanistan in 1972 and 1973, respectively, while the price paid to Iran was $0.307 per 1,000 c.f. for gas. . . . The total losses to Afghanistan (gains to the Soviet Union) for the two years were respectively $13.058 million and $11.363 million."[70] Afghanistan's trade with the Soviet Union increased during the first, second, and third Five-Year Plans, while the country's trade with the U.S. declined during the same period (see Table 2.4).

The country was in deep socioeconomic and political crisis.

The debt repayments were running at some $7 million annually, but within five years annual repayments on earlier debts rose to $25 million—equivalent to over 30 percent of total export earnings at the time. Almost two thirds of repayments were due to the Soviet Union, the chief creditor.[71]

The pro-U.S. and pro-Soviet social forces within and outside the state apparatus were dissatisfied with the ineffective leadership of King Zahir. Each was viewing internal and external conditions to topple the monarchy. A military coup by several political rivals of King Zahir (Mohammad Daoud, Abdul Wali son-in-law of King Zahir, former Prime Ministers Mohammad Hashim Maiwandwal and Mohammad Musa Shafiq) was about to occur. The last few years of King Zahir's rule coincided with national starvation, impoverishment, inflation, and disease. A World Bank report of 1972 graphically described the situation as follows:

Table 2.4
Afghanistan's Trade with U.S. and USSR, 1957–1972 (in millions of dollars)

Item	Country	Year			Total
		1st 5-Y Plan 1957—1961	2nd 5-Y Plan 1963—1967	3rd 5-Y Plan 1968—1972	
Exports	USA	52.9	45.5	5.6	104.0
	USSR	73.3	105.8	22.1	201.2
Imports	USA	27.4	24.3	2.3	54.0
	USSR	69.7	69.9	18.7	158.3

Source: Ministry of Planning, *Majmuaei-Aisayawi-e-Sali 1350* [Statistical dictionary of 1971] (Kabul: Matbaa-e-Dawlati, 1350, [1971]), p. 87.

The past fifteen years have been frustrating and disappointing for those concerned with the development in Afghanistan. A relatively large volume of aid
sustained high levels of investment to little visible purpose in terms of higher
standards of living for the majority of the population. To some extent it was
inevitable that the major share of investment would be needed for basic economic
and social infrastructure, with long gestation periods. However, it has proved
difficult to move from this stage to the point where effective use can be made
of the infrastructure created and a proper impetus can be provided to the kind
of productive activities which result in wider spread increases in income.

The report continued:

The responsibility for this situation lies with the inadequacies of administrative
structure. This is reflected in the failure of the government to manage the large
number of public enterprises efficiently, to allocate funds within projects so as
to secure the maximum return, to gear up its administrative capacity to prepare
new projects and to promote the institutional and legislative changes needed to
create an appropriate environment for private agricultural and industrial development.[72]

The economic crisis and mass starvation, on the one hand, and the
mass movement of the blue-collar workers and the internal struggle
within the ruling class on the other hand, paved the way for Soviet-
educated elites and the bourgeoisie (those favoring trade with the USSR)
concentrated around former Premier Mohammad Daoud to seize state
power through a military coup on 17 July 1973, and proclaim the country
a republic.

NOTES

1. Vartan Gregorian, *The Emergence of Modern Afghanistan: Politics of
Reform and Modernization* (Palo Alto: Stanford University Press, 1969), p.
370.

2. Ibid., p. 370.

3. Akhgar (Sazmani Mubariza Bara-e-Azadi Tabaqa-e-Kargar or Organization for Liberation of Working Class), *Afghanistan* (Tehran: 1980), p. 57.

4. National Intelligence Estimate (NIE-3), in Declassified Documents 6
(Washington, D.C., 1980), 80 (1950) no. 226A.

5. U.S. Department of State, *Foreign Relations of the United States 1949*
(Washington, D.C.: Government Printing Office, 1977), vol. 6, pp. 6–7.

6. Reardon J. Patrick, "Modernization and Reform: The Contemporary

Endeavor," in *Afghanistan: Some New Approaches* (Ann Arbor: The University of Michigan, 1969), pp. 153–54.

7. Henry S. Bradsher, *Afghanistan and the Soviet Union* (Durham: Duke University Press, 1983, 1985), p. 27; W. Joshua and S. P. Gilbert, eds., *Arms for the Third World: Soviet Military Aid Diplomacy* (Baltimore: Johns Hopkins University Press, 1969), p. 56.

8. *The Military Balance 1977–78* (London: International Institute of Strategic Studies, 1978), p. 55; Central Intelligence Agency (hereafter CIA), National Foreign Assessment Center, "Communist Aid to Less Developed Countries of the Free World, 1977: A Research Paper," (Washington, D.C.: November, 1978), p. 35.

9. John Scherer, *U.S.S.R. Facts and Figures Annual 1981* (Gulf Breeze: Academic International Press, 1981), vol. 5, pp. 258–59.

10. Bruce Amstutz, *Afghanistan: The First Five Years of Soviet Occupation* (Washington, D.C.: National Defense University, 1986), p. 21.

11. Louis Dupree, *Afghanistan* (Princeton: Princeton University Press, 1973).

12. *Nida-e-Khalq*, (Kabul) 26 February 1952.

13. Yu V. Gankovsky et al., *A History of Afghanistan* (Moscow: Progress Publishers, 1982), p. 247.

14. Afghanistan, *The Kabul Times Annual 1967* (Kabul: The Kabul Times Publishing Agency, 1967), p. 13.

15. Hafizullah Emadi, "Afghanistan's Struggle for National Liberation," *Studies in Third World Societies* 27 (March 1984):29.

16. Reardon J. Patrick, op. cit., p. 166.

17. Hakim Ziyaee, "Educational Development Projects Under Second Five-Year Plan and Future Long-Term Plan," *Afghanistan* 18 (October-November-December 1963):16.

18. Afghanistan, op. cit., p. 40.

19. Ibid., p. 40.

20. William W. Bechhoefer, "Architectural Education in Afghanistan," *Afghanistan Journal* (vol. 4, no. 4, 1977):48.

21. Louis Dupree, "A Note on Afghanistan: 1971," *AUFS Reports* 15 (July 1971):23.

22. USAID correspondence dated 28 November 1986 (1,823 scholarships since 1958); The Asia Foundation correspondence dated 2 October 1986 (55 scholarships from 1968 to 1979); Institute of International Education (IIE), correspondence, 10 September 1986 (48 scholarships from 16 November 1977 to 31 October 1983); *East-West Center 1985 Annual Report*, p. 54 (101 scholarships from 1960 to 1985); 214 Afghan students received American Field Service (AFS) scholarships between 1963 to 1973, 160 Afghan students were awarded Fulbright grants between 1962 to 1973, and 60 American professors and scholars conducted research and teaching in Afghanistan. Louis Dupree,

"The Afghan-American Educational Commission: Ten Years of Binational Cooperation," *AUFS Reports* 17(1974):4–8.

23. *Area Handbook for Afghanistan*, DA Pamphlet no. 550-65 (Washington, D.C.: The American University, 1969), p. 230.

24. Ibid., p. 231.

25. Ibid., p. 235.

26. Afghanistan, op. cit., p. 42.

27. Louis Dupree, "A Note on Afghanistan: 1971," op. cit., p. 23.

28. John Scherer, *U.S.S.R. Facts and Figures Annual*, op. cit., 1987, vol. 2, p. 261.

29. "USSR and Third World," Central Asian Research Centre, London, 1985, vol. 15, no. 2, p. 4.

30. *Area Handbook for Afghanistan*, op. cit., pp. 231–37.

31. Marvin G. Weinbaum, "Foreign Assistance to Afghan Higher Education," *Afghanistan Journal* (vol. 3, no. 3, 1976):84.

32. Louis Dupree, *Afghanistan*, op. cit., p. 484.

33. Ibid., pp. 503–4.

34. Ibid., p. 504.

35. Surkha (Sazmani Rahayi Bakhshi Khalqa-e-Afghanistan or Organization for Liberation of the People of Afghanistan), *Chegunagi-e- Paidayish wa Rushdi Bourgeoisie dar Afghanistan* [The process and development of bourgeoisie in Afghanistan] (Kabul: Ayendagan Press, 1980), p. 111.

36. Akhgar, op. cit. p. 15.

37. Louis Dupree, *Afghanistan*, op. cit., p. 507.

38. Leonid Teplinsky, "Soviet-Afghan Cooperation: Lenin's Behest Implemented," in *Afghanistan: Past and Present* (Moscow: U.S.S.R. Academy of Sciences, Oriental Studies in the U.S.S.R., no. 3, 1981), p. 209.

39. Ibid., p. 210.

40. *A Short Information About the Peoples Democratic Party of Afghanistan* (Kabul: Government Printing House, 1978).

41. Fazil M. Nazaar, "Development, Modernization and Leadership Style in Afghanistan: A Human Simulation in Politics," (Ph.D diss., Honolulu, University of Hawaii-Manoa, 1972), p. 63.

42. Louis Dupree, "Afghanistan and the Unpaved Road to Democracy," *Royal Central Asian Journal* 6 (October 1969):276.

43. Louis Dupree, "A Note on Afghanistan: 1971," *AUFS Reports* 15 (July 1971):17.

44. Akhgar, op. cit., p. 43.

45. U.S. Congress, House Committee on Foreign Affairs Hearing, *Mutual Security Programme*, 82d Cong., 1st sess. (Washington, D.C., 1951), p. 996.

46. Surkha, op. cit., pp. 168–69.

47. Ibid., p. 169.

48. Marvin Brant, "Recent Economic Development," in *Afghanistan in the 1970s*, Louis Dupree and Albert Linette, eds. (New York: Praeger Publishers, 1974), p. 94.

49. Surkha, op. cit., p. 168.

50. Cited in Surkha, p. 179.

51. Surkha, op. cit., p. 169.

52. U.S., *Foreign Relations of the United States 1949*, op. cit., p. 29.

53. U.S., *Foreign Relations of the United States 1951*, 1977, vol. 6, p. 2,012.

54. U.S. Department of Commerce, *Report to the U.S. Department of Commerce: U.S. Trade Mission to Afghanistan*, 20 August-10 September 1960, p. 5.

55. Afghanistan, Ministry of Planning, *Majmuaei Aisayawi-e-Sali 1350* [Statistical dictionary of 1971] (Kabul: Matbaa-e-Dawlati, 1350 [1971]), p. 161.

56. Louis Dupree, "American Private Enterprise in Afghanistan: The Investment Climate, Particularly as It Relates to One Company," *AUFS Reports* 4 (December 1960):15.

57. Nikita Khrushchev, *Khrushchev Remembers* (Boston: Little, Brown, 1970), pp. 507–8.

58. "Speeches by N. A. Bulganin at a Dinner in Kabul, 16 December 1955," in *N. S. Khrushchev Speeches During Sojourn in India, Burma and Afghanistan* (New Delhi: New Age Printing Press, 1956), p. 175.

59. Reardon J. Patrick, "Modernization and Reform: The Contemporary Endeavor," in *Afghanistan: Some New Approaches* (Ann Arbor: The University of Michigan, 1969), p. 168.

60. Afghanistan, op. cit., p. 51.

61. Ibid.

62. Ghulam Omar Saleh, "The Economical Geography of Afghanistan," *Afghanistan* 19 (January-February-March 1964):16.

63. Akhgar, op. cit., p. 43.

64. Afghanistan, Ministry of Planning, *Survey of Progress 1967–68* (Kabul: Government Printing House, 1968).

65. Afghanistan, Ministry of Planning, *Majmuaei Aisayawi-e-Sali 1350*, op. cit., p. 161.

66. Ghulam Omar Saleh, op. cit., p. 17.

67. Afghanistan, Royal Afghan Embassy in London, *Afghanistan News* 6 (January 1963):11.

68. John F. Shroder, Jr., "Afghanistan's Unsung Riches" *Christian Science Monitor*, 11 February 1982.

69. John F. Shroder, Jr., "The USSR and Afghanistan Mineral Resources," *Occasional Papers*, no. 3, University of Nebraska-Omaha, Reprint from *International Minerals* (Boulder: Westview Press, 1983), p. 121.

70. M. S. Noorzoy, "Long-Term Economic Relations Between Afghanistan and the Soviet Union: An Interpretive Study," *International Journal of Middle Eastern Studies* 17 (May 1985):161.

71. Anthony Hyman, *Afghanistan Under Soviet Domination 1964–83* (New York: St. Martin's Press, 1984), p. 34.

72. World Bank, *Afghanistan: The Journey to Economic Development* vol. 1, The Main Report no. 1777a-AF (17 March 1978), pp. 28–29.

3 State and the Superpowers

THE EMERGENCE OF A REPUBLICAN STATE: 1973

On 17 July 1973 President Mohammad Daoud delivered a speech to the nation. He justified the overthrow of the monarchy on the grounds that during the decade of constitutional experience (1963–73):

Democracy or the government of the people was changed into anarchy and the constitutional monarchy to a despotic regime. All these forces struggled against one another and the people, and in pursuing the principle of divide and rule, fire was lighted throughout the country. So in this turbulent and dark atmosphere impregnated with misery, poverty, and misfortune they [the ruling class and official bureaucrats] were able to attain their material and political ends. The patriots, wherever they were, watched with deep sorrow and anguish this horrible state of their nation. But they were constantly aware of the situation, especially the Afghan armed forces who felt this agony more than anyone else exercising extreme patience hoping that today or tomorrow the vile and rotten system in Afghanistan would become aware of the misery of the nation and endeavor to reform itself. But the result proved that these hopes are impertinent, and the regime and system became so corrupt that no hope or expectation for its reform existed. Consequently all patriots, especially the patriotic armed forces of Afghanistan, decided to put an end to this rotten system and deliver the nation from their plight . . . the system has been overthrown and a new order which is the republican regime has been established which conforms to the true spirit of Islam.[1]

Progressive social forces and a broad section of concerned citizens remained critical of the situation and of President Daoud's leadership. To many of these people the transfer of power from one member of the royal family to the other was not a solution to Afghanistan's under-development. The pro-Soviet intellectuals welcomed and celebrated the emergence of a republican order. Noor Mohammad Taraki, General Secretary of the People's Democratic Party of Afghanistan (PDPA), *Khalq* faction, reflected on the party's support to the republican regime of President Daoud on the grounds that,

we thought that maybe Daoud will already take some action in the interest of the oppressed class of people. . . . He delivered a speech called "Address to the Nation" which, compared to the objectives of the monarchical regime, was progressive. We were satisfied with this speech and we were right in supporting Daoud in the light of this speech.[2]

Domestic Policy

In order to consolidate his social base of power President Daoud eliminated eminent opposition leaders. Former Premier Mohammad Hashim Maiwandwal was arrested and a few days later it was announced that he committed suicide in prison. President Daoud also arrested civilian and army officers associated with Maiwandwal. Of the 45 persons who were arrested in this connection several were executed while others received jail sentences ranging from two years to life. President Daoud arrested Ghulam Mohammad Niazi, leader of the known *Eikh-wan-ul-Muslimin* (Islamic Brotherhood), and his followers on charges that they were involved in sabotaging activities against the state. President Daoud also had other influential persons such as a well-known merchant, Mohammad Arif, known as Arif Rikshaw, put to death and nationalized the properties of another merchant, Hazargul.

President Daoud appointed to his cabinet army officers of both Khalq and Parcham factions of the PDPA who had played a major role in the July coup and also promoted the lower ranking officials of the army, *Khurdzabitan* (petty officers), to the rank of permanent lieutenant with no further promotion possible, so as to secure the armed force's confidence in him as a perpetuator of the new bureaucratic state system—the republic. President Daoud tried to further strengthen the new regime's social bases by prohibiting political parties of the opposition forces and dispatching young members of Parcham and Khalq factions of the PDPA to the countryside to propagate the policies of the state among the people. President Daoud believed that by sending young members of the PDPA to the provinces he would prevent the possibility of a countercoup.[3]

To expand his base of power, President Daoud tried to win over the intelligentsia and students to support his policies. For this reason he initiated educational reform on the basis of which students enrolled in grades one through three were automatically promoted without annual examination and primary schools upgraded from six to eight years. After completing eight years of primary school the students had to sit for entrance examinations to high schools. According to the reform, all religious and public schools and institutions of higher education (universities) were directed and administered by the Ministry of Education. Rectors, professors, teachers, and employees of educational establishments were all selected and appointed by the state.[4]

To improve the country's economy President Daoud announced he would nationalize the banking system. As a result of this nationalization policy the privately owned and largest commercial enterprise, the *Bank-e-Milli-e-Afghanistan* or the National Bank of Afghanistan and its several foreign branches, as well as its establishments throughout Afghanistan, came under state control.[5] A major aspect of the development policy adopted by the leadership during this period was state intervention in economic development by imposing capitalism on industry "from above" without altering the precapitalist mode of production. As a result of this state intervention in economic activities the enormous trade-usurious profits which were appropriated by the Bank-e-Milli-e-Afghanistan and other banks in the private sectors such as the Pashtani Tejarati Bank, the Industrial Development Bank, the Agricultural Bank, and the Mortgage and Construction Bank were now being appropriated by the new bourgeoisie in power concentrated around President Mohammad Daoud.

President Daoud remembered past peasant uprisings and declared a land reform from the top in hopes of offering a panacea to the plight of the peasant population. His main goal in promising "land reform" and land distribution was, on the one hand, to stabilize the political situation by diverting the peasant movement and its further escalation and, on the other, to legitimize the new regime. The state declared it would distribute land from the state-owned lands to landless peasants and farmers. A year later the state claimed that 5,371 families received land, 3,930 in the Hilmand Valley, 1,269 in Nangarhar, and 172 in Ghorband. In other words approximately 32,226 individuals benefited from the project.[6] The state announced its nationwide land reform in July 1975 and promised to implement it by August 1976. The land reform

envisaged the maximum size holdings of 20 hectares for better lands and 40 hectares for poorer. Under the law the state redeemed surplus land from landowners over and above the established maximum on a deferred payment plan [over] the next twenty-five years, at two percent interest. The redeemed lands should be sold to landless peasants also on the deferred payment plan of twenty five years and at the same interest rate.[7]

The Rural Development Board was set up to study in detail the economic and social conditions in every village and to categorize the land into better and poorer grades. A board commission was sent to villages to promote the program and to mobilize the villagers for collective projects. The program failed for the following reasons: (a) Since the salaries of the state employees were far below their subsistence level, the commission members used this opportunity to supplement their incomes by taking bribes from landowners in registering their holdings below the two categories of land holdings. For example, during land registration, the officials in charge took bribes in the amount $200,000 from landowners in Uruzgan province.[8] (b) A great number of landowners, using their social influence, registered their estates in the names of a few of their relatives or other figureheads, and reduced the officially registered size of their holdings. Thus the state's land reform did not break the feudal relations of production and put an end to the exploitation of peasantry by feudal landowners. Thus the situation in the countryside remained as much a problem as before. This situation led to peasant and workers strikes and protest demonstrations in various parts of the country. To maintain stability President Daoud came down hard on the Bagrami Textile workers, workers of the National Bus Company, and the peasant movements in Paktiya, Laghman, Bamiyan, Parwan, and Badakhshan provinces, and imprisoned their leaders.

To strengthen his social base of power and establish himself as revolutionary leader President Daoud, who was cousin and brother-in-law to ex-King Mohammad Zahir, and known by the title of *Sardar* (the title for members of the royal family which means noble person) tried to distance himself from the royal family. He encouraged his supporters not to call him *Sardar* but by his first name, Daoud. President Daoud also tried to portray an iconoclastic impression by allowing antimonarchist political slogans during his first few months in office (in practice and behind the scenes), but he continued supporting the deposed King Zahir by sending monthly allowances to his family, exiled in Italy. "The King and Queen received $2,500 a month each plus $1,000 for each child and other close relatives—about $10,000 a month in all."[9]

President Daoud not only supported the exiled family of deposed King Zahir but also appointed distant members of his family (the Mohammadzai dynasty) to key government offices. The top posts in the executive and the judiciary in the state were reserved for certain members of the Mohammadzai dynasty. The Ministry of Foreign Affairs was administered entirely by the Mohammadzai family. For instance, of 21 ambassadors, ministers, and consul generals assigned abroad in the early period of Daoud's presidency, 16 of them were Mohammadzai.[10]

In order to create a legitimate base for the state, in March 1977 President Daoud called the *Loya Jirgah*—Grand Assembly of Tribal Leaders. He appointed 130 selected personages including military officers, factory workers, small farmers, urban intellectuals, and women in order to display the democratic character of the assembly, and got this assembly to pass a new constitution. The grand assembly elected him president of the country as well as prime minister, defense minister, and supreme commander of the armed forces.[11]

Social forces loyal to President Daoud began portraying him as a national leader and the founding father of a republican order in Afghanistan. President Daoud's pictures were displayed everywhere, in public places as well as government offices and private houses. The state-controlled media also began propagating Daoud's policies both at home and abroad. The constitution adopted by the Loya Jirgah was a replica of an authoritarian state's document that provided for a presidential system of government within the framework of a single-party system. The constitution enabled President Daoud to legalize his National Revolution Party (*Hizbi Enqilab-e-Milli*) as the only political party in Afghanistan.

Neither President Daoud's new constitution nor his economic development projects put an end to the rampant unemployment and exploitation of the peasantry by feudal landowners, or the general misery of the population. The country's trade deficit was growing bigger. For instance, the 1973–74 trade deficit of $35.2 million rose to $41.2 million in 1975–76. The cost of living rose from 97 percent to 111 percent in 1974 and to 129 percent in 1975.[12] This situation was sowing massive waves of dissatisfaction among merchants, blue-collar workers, intellectuals, and the peasants. To prevent the development of a social revolution the state eased travel restrictions for people to leave the country. On the basis of such a policy a great number of blue-collar workers from both urban and rural areas were allowed to migrate to the Persian Gulf states in search of employment. During the first two years of the republican regime almost one million laborers emigrated from the country, most of them going to Iran.[13]

Foreign Affairs

During the early years of his rule President Daoud maintained a pro-Soviet orientation in his foreign policy. He endorsed the Soviet Union's plan for an Asian "Collective Security" arrangement,[14] and turned down a suggestion by the shah of Iran, who was encouraged by the United States, to have Afghanistan join the Regional Cooperation for Development (RCD) formed by Pakistan, Iran, and Turkey in 1964, intended to unite South Asian countries in a strong economic community.[15]

President Daoud continued his anti-Iran policies and arrested former Prime Minister Mohammad Musa Shafiq, charging him with bribery because he had earlier signed the Hilmand River Treaty with Iran. The proclamation of Afghanistan as a republic and its Soviet-oriented policy as well as its continuous "socialist" and "revolutionary" agitation were seen as a threat to the U.S. sphere of influence in the region.

The pro-U.S. shah of Iran, regarded as the best ally safeguarding U.S. interests in the Middle East, considered President Daoud's anti-monarchist and "revolutionary" agitation a threat to political stability in Iran and tried to force the leadership in Afghanistan to revise its policy toward Iran. To achieve this the shah resorted to use of force and initiated a calculated raid on Afghan military posts on the Afghanistan-Iran border which resulted in the death of 70 Afghan soldiers.[16]

In the meantime the shah also ordered the deportation of approximately one million Afghan laborers from Iran. A great number of laborers who returned to Afghanistan were unable to find employment and the state could not provide any kind of accommodation to them. The situation was threatening the regime in Kabul. In an attempt to prevent the possibility of social unrest, President Daoud tried to normalize the country's relations with Iran so that the Iranian leadership would allow Afghan laborers to return and work there. For this reason President Daoud sent his brother Mohammad Naim to Tehran to normalize the relations between the two countries.

Following President Daoud's personal emissary's visit to Tehran, relations between Afghanistan and Iran were greatly improved. Afghan laborers who left Iran were allowed to return and work in Iran. In October 1974 the shah also promised to provide $2 billion in economic aid over a period of ten years to Afghanistan. The most important item of the aid package was the construction of a railroad from Kabul to Mashhad, Iran, which would provide Afghanistan with a trade route through Iranian ports.

As relations between the two countries improved, Afghanistan agreed to purchase 70,000 tons of diesel fuel and 10,000 tons of kerosene from the National Iranian Oil Company.[17] In the meantime, Iran also agreed to participate in the construction of sugar, cement, wool, and cotton textiles and paper plants in various provinces as well as in development of water resources and agriculture in the lower Hilmand basin[18] and committed itself to provide $10 million to the newly established Export Promotion Bank of Afghanistan.[19] The Iranian government also took a keen interest in improving Afghanistan's transportation networks and agreed to provide 200 buses and 180 minibuses.[20]

The relationship between Afghanistan and Iran was further strengthened when President Daoud visited Iran in 1976. As a result of Iran's economic assistance to Afghanistan, President Daoud made a considerable shift in his domestic and foreign policies. During his third year in office President Daoud strengthened the country's relations with Western countries and also showed a great interest in joining the Regional Cooperation for Development (RCD).[21]

Relations with Pakistan and the Question of Pushtunistan

The fate of Pushtunistan remained a touchy issue between the ruling class of both Afghanistan and Pakistan since the partition of the Indian subcontinent into Pakistan and India in 1947. The emerging bourgeoisie within the leadershp position in Afghanistan have sought access to the sea to facilitate their business dealings. Their claim to defend the rights of self-determination for the Pushtun people in Pakistan's North West Frontier Province (NWFP) known as Pushtunistan, was prompted by their desire to gain access to the Arabian Sea. Premier Mohammad Hashim, during an interview given in Bombay, expressed his opinion on the subject:

If an independent Pushtunistan cannot be set up, the frontier province should join Afghanistan. Our neighbour Pakistan will realize that our country with its population and trade, needs an outlet to the sea, which is very essential . . . if the nations of the world desire peace and justice, . . . it will be easy for us to get an outlet to the sea.[22]

Since then the issue of Pushtunistan has remained a major factor in Afghanistan foreign policy vis-à-vis Pakistan. The leadership in Afghanistan wanted to annex Pushtunistan to Afghanistan but they were not in a position to implement it in practice. Thus they continued supporting the cause of the Pushtunistan people (at least in words). Another reason the leadership in Afghanistan supported the issue of Pushtunistan was to divert public opinion away from domestic problems and the crisis of legitimacy within the country. The government of Afghanistan during Daoud's premiership, (1953–1963) attached great importance to the issue to the extent that both Afghanistan and Pakistan passed the level of political accusation and began mobilizing their armed forces across a common border, the Durand Line. But following the resignation of Premier Daoud in 1963 political tension between the two countries was eased; however, Afghanistan support of the issue of Pushtunistan remained at the diplomatic level.

When Daoud seized state and political power in 1973 he again announced his support for the cause of the Pushtun people of Pakistan. In an address to the nation he admitted that the Durand Line, which divided the Pushtun population between Afghanistan and Pakistan, remained an obstacle in maintaining a friendly relationship with Pakistan. President Daoud took the matter so seriously that on 5 November 1973, his deputy Foreign Minister Waheed Abdullah declared that Afghanistan did not recognize the Durand Line as an official border line between the two countries since it separates almost 2.5 million Pushtuns from Afghanistan.

The leadership in Afghanistan maintained a hostile policy toward Pakistan and accused the latter of suppressing the national aspirations of the Pushtun and Baluch people for autonomy and independence. When the leadership in Pakistan requested military and economic assistance from the United States, President Daoud saw such assistance to Pakistan as a threat to the balance of power between Afghanistan and Pakistan. During a visit to India President Daoud expressed his government's concern over the issue.

[T]he lifting of arms embargo to Pakistan by the United States government in a time that Pakistan is engaged in shedding blood in Baluchistan and Pushtunistan has caused grave concern to the people of Afghanistan. It will lead to imbalance in the region and promote an armaments race and would create an additional threat to the peace in the region.[23]

President Daoud's policy of supporting the rights to self-determination of the Pushtun people of Pakistan worried President Zulfiqar Ali Bhutto and compelled him to take measures to try and force President Daoud to sit at a negotiating table with the leadership in Pakistan. To this end President Bhutto established an anti-Kabul propaganda center in Pakistan and gave sanctuary to opponents to Daoud such as Gulbuddin Hikmatyar, head of the Islamic Party, and Burhanuddin Rabbani, head of the Islamic Society.

In addition, President Bhutto ordered the construction of roads in North-West Frontier Province (NWFP) to advance Pakistan's military capability in maintaining stability in the region in the event that the government of Afghanistan supports a Pushtun uprising in the region. President Bhutto's

drive toward superficial modernization of the Tribal Areas was clearly prompted by the overthrow of the monarchy in neighboring Afghanistan. It was part of a strategic military offensive designed to de-stabilize Daoud. That is why the Razmak camp in South Waziristan was reactivated, and that also explains the desperate rush to construct new roads and improve communications. The high command in Islamabad was determined to forestall a "Pathandesh" on its northern frontiers. Bhutto's forward policy was designed, by putting maximum pressure on Kabul, to permanently foreclose the Pushtunistan issue. A tribal revolt which erupted on 21 July 1975 in the Panjshir Valley north of Kabul was planned and executed by Afghan exiles financed and armed by Islamabad.[24]

President Bhutto's policy of supporting the opposition forces within Afghanistan (the Islamic fundamentalists) further destabilized the situation in Afghanistan. President Daoud was not in a position to retaliate in kind. This led him to once again consider normalization of relations between the two countries. President Daoud believed that a friendly relationship with Pakistan would allow him to consolidate his position. Therefore, he was looking for an opportunity to open a dialogue with the leadership of Pakistan. It was during this period that the shah of Iran acted as a mediator between the two countries. The role of the shah was crucial in the normalization of relations between Afghanistan and Pakistan. Elaborating on Iran's effort, President Daoud said "we are deeply gratified for Iranian economic assistance to Afghanistan, and likewise we are thoughtful for the interest which Iran takes in eliminating tension between Afghanistan and Pakistan."[25] The relationship between Afghanistan and Pakistan improved to the extent that both President Daoud and Bhutto of Pakistan made an official visit to the other's country.

The Superpowers and President Mohammad Daoud

The Soviet Union was the first country to extend diplomatic recognition to the republican regime in Afghanistan. The Soviet leaders pledged to provide political and economic assistance to the country. A year later President Daoud was invited for a friendly visit to the Soviet Union. During his visit the Soviet government agreed to participate in Afghanistan's economic development projects such as irrigation, power generation, construction of a copper smelting plant, expansion of the chemical fertilizer industry, a thermal power plant, construction of a silo, gin and textile mills, installation of a carrier radio-telephone system between Kabul and Mazari Sharif, a laboratory for analysis of minerals, construction of airports as well as several other projects. The Soviet Union also agreed to defer the payment of 100 million rubles which it loaned Afghanistan under a technical and economic assistance agreement.[26]

In March 1974 a five-year barter protocol was signed between Afghanistan and the Soviet Union. On the basis of this protocol Afghanistan was to export olives, citrus fruits, raisins, honey, cement, and natural gas in return for machinery, sugar, petroleum products, and fertilizer. Afghanistan's export of natural gas to the Soviet Union began in October

Table 3.1

U.S. and USSR Economic Assistance to Afghanistan, 1973–1977 (in millions of dollars)

Country	1973	1974	Fourth Five-Year Plan 1975	1976	1977	Total
USA	33.0	16.4	19.3	12.0	9.1	89.8
USSR	428.0	—	600.0	3.6	—	1,031.6

Sources: U.S. US Agency for International Development, *Helping People* (Kabul: United States Embassy, April 1976), p. 35; *The Quarterly Economic Review* 1976, p. 18; 1977, p. 17; 1975, p. 21; 1976, p. 18.

1967 and by January 1977 approximately 23 billion cubic meters had been exported to the Soviet Union at a rate of ca 2.8 billion cubic meters annually (the export of natural gas constituted about 45 percent of Afghanistan's total exports to the Soviet Union).[27]

During the two years of President Daoud's rule the Soviet Union extended a loan of $428 million for the survey and construction of development projects[28] and granted $600 million for financing a five-year development plan which had been launched in 1973[29] as well as a loan of $3.6 million worth of geological survey and exploration equipment, agricultural machinery, and construction equipment (see Table 3.1).[30] Soviet military assistance to Afghanistan in 1977 included a few significant new weapons such as the SA-3 and SA-7 surface-to-air missiles.[31]

Although the United States was dismayed with President Daoud's socioeconomic strategies and close relationship with the Soviet Union, it extended diplomatic recognition to the republican regime. The U.S. administration viewed Afghanistan's close ties with the Soviet Union as a threat to the political stability in South Asia and the Middle East. The U.S. concern over Afghanistan's hostility toward its two allies, Pakistan and Iran, was reflected in a top U.S. memo by the Department of State:

Daoud's cordial relations with the U.S.S.R. may jeopardize the ratification of a pending treaty on the apportionment of the waters of the Hilmand River, as well as the access to road and port facilities that the Shah has promised to Afghanistan. The Shah is likely to view any threat to Pakistan's unity as a threat to Iran.[32]

In order to thwart Soviet influence and encourage Afghanistan to distance herself from the Soviet Union and its bloc, Theodore L. Eliot, Jr., former U.S. ambassador to Afghanistan, advised the Department of State that the United States must continue providing economic assistance to Afghanistan as a means to this end. A top secret memo from the U.S. embassy in Kabul to the Department of State reads: "We continue to demonstrate our friendly and tangible interest through a visible American presence in this country."[33]

In order to exert its influence the United States continued its development projects and offered financial aid to Afghanistan's modernization projects. Three U.S. firms also concluded an agreement to build a $51 million, 1,000 ton-per-day cement plant in Kandahar province.[34] The leading U.S. export to Afghanistan was used clothing, totalling about $900,000. According to the *Wall Street Journal* "the influx of old clothes here has all but killed Afghanistan's age-old hand-loom industry. The more expensive homespun clothes simply cannot compete with the cheap machine-sewn foreign castoffs that seem to herald the first invasion of western imperialism into this remote land."[35] According to available statistics the total U.S. economic assistance during the period of 1973–1978 was estimated to be approximately $89.8 million (see Table 3.1).[36]

As the result of the U.S. economic assistance the relations between the two countries improved. According to the U.S. administration:

U.S.-Afghan relations during 1977 were excellent. The government of Afghanistan (GOA) fulfilled an obligation to U.S. to establish a joint commission to control narcotic production and trafficking. Daoud accepted an invitation to make a state visit to the U.S. in the Summer 1978. Funding for the U.S. military training program for Afghan officers was doubled in an effort to offset—albeit to a modest degree—the massive Soviet predominance in the area of foreign support for the Afghan armed forces.[37]

Conservative religious leaders, liberal social forces, and Islamic fundamentalists were not happy with President Daoud's association with members of the pro-Soviet People's Democratic Party of Afghanistan, PDPA. They began to oppose the government policies both at home and abroad. The growing social opposition inside the country and political pressures and economic incentives from abroad (U.S. and Iran) finally pushed the leadership in Afghanistan to distance the country from the Soviet Union and its bloc.

During the last two years of his rule President Daoud made a noticeable shift in his policies that indicated a desire to reduce Afghanistan dependence on the Soviet Union and its bloc. For instance, President Daoud began sending more military officers and students to Egypt and India for training and increased the number of students going to the United States. President Daoud further decided to upgrade the existing military academy in Kabul so as to be able to award "war degrees" to military officers who formally got such degrees from abroad.[38] The number of students who studied in the Soviet Union between 1972 and 1975 declined in comparison to those in the United States (412 Afghan students awarded scholarships to the U.S. and 384 to the Soviet Union).[39] President Daoud strengthened Afghanistan's relations with Western and "nonaligned" countries and began to advocate a "nonalignment" policy.

Contradictions between the pro-Soviet and pro-U.S. social forces within the state apparatus was growing rapidly over many issues, and increased further after President Daoud strengthened Afghanistan's relations with the West. Members and supporters of the PDPA armed forces were heading toward a clash with President Daoud. To consolidate his base of power, President Daoud began to purge members of the PDPA from the government agencies and tried to rehabilitate the monarchists and rightists by appointing them to high government positions.

The PDPA members who held cabinet posts within the state apparatus (Minister of Interior Faiz Mohammad, Minister of Frontier Affairs Pacha Gul Wafadar, Minister of Communications Abdul Hamid Muhtat, and Deputy Premier Mohammad Hassan Sharq) along with other high-ranking officers both in the army and civil administrations were expelled from the bureaucracy and began raising their voices in opposition to President Daoud and his supporters. Afghan students supporting a Soviet political and ideological orientation in Afghanistan described the situation in Afghanistan and President Daoud's policy:

Signing contracts with the imperialist countries runs counter to the interest of Afghanistan's economy and independence. Advocating a passive policy toward

the Pushtunistan question damages the interest of the Pushtun people. . . . These are concrete evidences showing that the reactionary forces have
consolidated their positions within the state apparatus and deliberately prevent
the country's socio-economic development.[40]

President Daoud visited Moscow in January 1977 to explain his government's policies to the Soviet leadership. The Soviet Union's dis-
pleasure with President Daoud's policies grew and was angrily expressed
during a meeting between President Daoud and Secretary General of
the Communist Party of the Soviet Union Leonid Brezhnev in Moscow.
In a brief, hostile exchange, Brezhnev told President Daoud to expel
all imperialist advisors from Afghanistan.[41] This provoked President
Daoud's anger to the extent that he slammed his fist on the conference
table and told Secretary General Brezhnev that the people of Afghanistan
were masters of their own house and no foreign country could tell them
how to run their own affairs.[42]

As the relationship between Afghanistan and the Soviet Union de-
teriorated, the two factions of the People's Democratic Party of Afghanistan (PDPA), *Khalq* (the People), and *Parcham* (the Flag) agreed to
reunite and form a single party in the early summer of 1977. It is believed
that the Communist Party of India acted as a mediator.[43] It was at this
time that President Daoud tried to further strengthen Afghanistan's relations with Western countries and visited Saudi Arabia and Kuwait in
April 1978. When President Daoud returned home from his last visit
abroad, he did not use any leftist-oriented terminology as he had at the
beginning of his three years of rule; instead he talked about Afghan
nationalism and national pride. President Daoud started attacking his
opponents and referring to their ideology as "imported ideology."

President Daoud's pro-Western policy antagonized the PDPA as well
as the Soviet Union. Contradictions between the state and the PPDA
grew and intensified. It was during this period that Mir Akbar Khayber,
a leading ideologue of the Parcham faction of the PDPA, was assassinated on 17 April 1978. President Daoud ordered the army and police
forces to maintain a state of readiness in case PDPA members and
supporters began to engage in sabotaging activities. During Khayber's
funeral on 19 April 1978, the PDPA members and loyalists staged a
large-scale anti-U.S. demonstration in Kabul. This gave President
Daoud an excuse to arrest the PDPA leadership, Noor Mohammad

Taraki, Hafizullah Amin, and Babrak Karmal a week later. However, he did not arrest PDPA members in the Afghan armed forces.

The state of military readiness provided an opportunity to military officers of the PDPA within the army to execute the preplanned coup on 28 April 1978.[44] By the end of the month the PDPA leaders had been released and Afghanistan was proclaimed a democratic republic with Noor Mohammad Taraki as president of the country.

THE BIRTH OF A DEMOCRATIC STATE: 1978

Consolidation of State Hegemony

Noor Mohammad Taraki, General Secretary of the People's Democratic Party of Afghanistan (PDPA) and head of the state, described the circumstances prior to the *Saur* (April) military coup that brought about the downfall of President Daoud and his five-year republican order in these words:

Daoud deceitfully and with Machiavellian approaches concentrated state power in his person and at the beginning in a bid to deceive and beguile the public declared a relatively progressive program which was supported by the progressive forces. But in five years practically no change took place in the direction of social and economic progress of the country. Remnants of decayed monarchy and corrupt bureaucracy and the torture machine of the monarchical order and the ruling despotic and exploiting strata lived and endured in the country. The band of the royal family of Mohammad Nadir, inside and outside the country in collusion with internal and external enemies of Afghanistan, continued with their treacherous royal intrigues . . . with the purge of national and progressive elements from state positions Mohammad Daoud, after a short time, practically entered into unity with rightists, reactionary, royalist elements. . . . Mohammad Daoud . . . was ready to sacrifice the interest of the nation . . . in his treacherous political gamblings. . . . The foreign policy of Daoud's regime assumed increasingly the form of dealing, collusion and surrender to imperialism, reaction and attachment to it.[45]

The pro-Western policy of President Daoud indeed antagonized the PDPA and its mentor the Soviet Union and caused the former to mobilize its forces within the army to topple President Daoud and seize the state apparatus. Noor Mohammad Taraki stated that when Daoud attacked us and treacherously put us into prison, our comrades in the armed forces according to our previous instructions issued to the responsible liaison member launched the resurrection in broad daylight, destroying forever the decayed Daoud regime and replacing it with the present Khalqi government.[46]

To legitimize the Saur military coup the leadership justified it as a bona fide revolution that was based on the principle of socialist revolution. President Taraki writes:

If the Great October Socialist Revolution in 1917 rocked the whole world, the Great Saur Revolution, which triumphed with the inspiration of the Great October Revolution, also jolted all the toiling people of the world and drew their best wishes. It was particularly an example for the developing countries to liberate their own toilers from the oppression of exploiters and to wrap up vestiges of imperialism and reaction.[47]

Elaborating on this point, Premier Amin writes:

The leadership had realized that it would take a long time to follow the classical way of wresting the political power by the working class as this called for toppling the government simultaneously with the crushing of the Afghan army, creating a new revolutionary one. . . . [It] was even impossible for many years to come. . . . Finally, under the leadership of the PDPA and with the participation of the officers and soldiers of the armed forces who were party members . . . the Afghan version of proletarian revolution started at nine in the morning of the 7th of Saur (April) and ended at seven in the evening the same day.[48]

Premier Amin portrayed the *Saur* ''revolution'' as a model for other backward countries. He writes: ''prior to our 'revolution' the working classes everywhere wanted to follow in the footprints of the Great October Socialist Revolution. However, after the Great April (Saur) Revolution the toilers should know that there does exist a shortcut which can transfer power from the feudal class to the working class and our revolution proved it.''[49]

Lacking a social base and public recognition before and after the April military coup, the PDPA did everything possible to publicly promote President Taraki as a national leader above all previous leaders. The PDPA went so far as to say that President Taraki's titles from the ''Leader of the Revolution to the Genius of the East''—would take up a paragraph in newspapers and journals. The party and Taraki were considered to be one by party members. Premier Amin writes: "Party and Taraki are body and soul, can body be separated from soul? When we speak of party, we speak of Taraki, when we speak of Taraki, we speak of party."[50]

The PDPA claimed that the new state was a "democratic" state that represented the "genuine" interests of the oppressed strata of the country—workers, peasants, and national bourgeoisie. In order to legitimize the state, the PDPA abrogated the old constitution, promised to draft a new one, and announced an 11-point charter of rules and orders to govern the country under the guidance of the "Democratic Revolutionary Council."

To expand its social base, the state readmitted 25,000 eighth-grade graduates into high schools who could not secure admission in the past because of educational reforms initiated by then President Daoud. For the same reason the state issued an order for the release of 5,500 prisoners from prisons throughout the country,[51] but soon filled all the prisons with new prisoners; according to Amnesty International's representative who visited Afghanistan, there were 12,000 political prisoners alone in the Puli Charkhi prison in Kabul between April 1978 and September 1979.[52]

To firmly control the repressive state apparatus the PDPA tried to restructure the armed forces and gendarmery by appointing party members and party sympathizers to key administrative posts and opening a political training course within the armed forces to imbue regular soldiers and cadets with the ruling ideology. The state under the direction of the PDPA dismissed most previous high-ranking officials, asked most previous ambassadors to resign their posts overseas, and dismissed all governors and district officers, replacing them with party members. The party also began purging doubtful elements within its ranks. As a result, inter-party struggle developed and culminated in the purge of the Parcham faction of the party headed by Babrak Karmal, vice president and prime minister, and most of its prominent members.

The party also attempted to display its revolutionary character by initiating reforms, launching exhibits of revolutionary signs and posters, and ordering people to paint the doors and windows of their houses red. The state and the party sought to transform the feudal mode of production by issuing decrees from above without the participation of the peasantry, blue-collar workers, and middle-income strata and issued various decrees forming the framework of their social policies. The most important are: Decree number 6, regarding the reduction of loans and mortgages, Decree number 7, related to women's emancipation and Decree number 8, regarding land reform.

Decree number 6 was designed to do away with feudal practices and to free the peasantry from feudal oppression. According to this decree those landless peasants or peasants holding 4.05 hectares of land were exempted from payment of debts and interest to landowners who mortgaged their land in 1353 (1974) or before. Decree number 7 advocated women's emancipation and placed a heavy restriction on the payment of *Mehr* (bride price) and other marriage-related expenses. The decree also defined a marriage age (16 for girls and 18 for boys), prohibited arranged marriages, and supported a woman's right to seek divorce. Decree number 8 limited the landholdings of feudal landowners to six hectares of better land, with the rest being subject to confiscation by the state.

The two decrees, numbers 6 and 8, in actuality did not break the power of feudal landowners because on the one hand the landowners had registered their land and property in the name of their sons and grandsons, and on the other the peasantry was not consciously and politically ready to seize lands from landowners, as they regarded the seizure of land from feudal landowners an illegal and immoral act that is not based on their religious beliefs. Even if they had done so, they were not in a position to take care of the land as they had no means at their disposal to plow, cultivate, and harvest the land. Thus objectively they remained dependent on feudal landowners. In some cases feudal landowners killed peasants who seized their land and displayed their bodies in public to intimidate other peasants from doing so; the state could not extend protection to landless peasants, and this caused the latter to reject the state decree in order to avoid bloodshed between immediate relatives and tribes.[53]

The "democratic" state also established the National Agency for the Campaign Against Illiteracy (NACAI). The main goal of the state was to inculcate a "proletarian" consciousness in the people to support the regime. Young party members forced old women and girls to attend night courses offered by the NACAI. The secret police raided houses at night in major cities to arrest members of the opposition groups. A few instances have been recorded in which women were abused. The ruling party officially denied all these charges as baseless propaganda by the opposition forces and "antirevolutionary" groups. President Taraki writes:

There has occurred only one event after the revolution in which a few thieves broke in a house and molested the family. So far we have not reached any agreement on what kind of punishment should be meted out to those thieves.[54]

Anyone who opposed the party line was branded a traitor or anti-revolutionary and tortured to death in Afghanistan's prisons. According to a report by Amnesty International on 16 November 1979, the Ministry of the Interior released a list of 12,000 names of mainly political prisoners who died in Kabul jails in the period after April 1978. According to the report, most of the victims were professors, teachers, students, civil servants, mullahs, shopkeepers, etc., including 800 children whose only crime was that they were relatives of political prisoners.[55] Women who petitioned on the whereabouts of their husbands were abused by the state officials and were told "go get a new husband" and fathers who asked about their sons were told "they have gone to the camp of antirevolutionaries in Pakistan."

The state's policy antagonized a great number of people and forced them to fight for the sake of their own survival and safety. The leadership in Kabul blamed religous leaders for instigating the public uprising against the state and declared their own "Jihad" against them. President Taraki writes: "In 1357 (1978) the people of Afghanistan declared jihad against Sheikhs (priests), clerics and Eikhwanis (Islamic Brotherhood) made in London and Paris and all our toiling Muslim people expressed hatred against them."[56]

Such a repressive policy (consolidating the Khalq's version of the "proletarian dictatorship") provoked antistate sentiment among a great number of the peasantry, intellectuals, and middle-income strata throughout the country and drove the oppressed and angry peasants (whom the regime was supposed to liberate) to the side of feudal land-owners in their fight against the state.

Crisis of Legitimation

Following the April 1978 military coup d'etat the Soviet Union was the first country to extend diplomatic recognition to Afghanistan and made a commitment to provide economic and military assistance. In

May 1978 the Soviets agreed to participate in 31 economic projects and in July 1978 it concluded an agreement for $250 million in military assistance. A year later, in August 1979, the Soviets announced a ten-year moratorium on the country's debt payments to the Soviet Union.

The Soviet Union also granted 10,000 scholarships for prospective students to study in the USSR. Soviet military advisors were dispatched to Afghanistan to reorganize and train the country's armed forces. The number of Soviet military technicians and advisors reached 4,000 prior to the Soviet military involvement in Afghanistan in December 1979.[57] The presence of Soviet military and technical advisors was so pervasive in every department in the state apparatus that state officials had to secure Soviet advisors' permission in handling daily bureaucratic affairs. This led many people to criticize the PDPA leadership as traitors who sold out the country to the Soviets. President Taraki justified the presence of Soviet advisors on the grounds that "the Soviet experts are large in numbers to some extent because they are economical for us. You see each of other [foreign] experts demands $2,000 to $2,500 or $3,000 as monthly salary but the salary of a Soviet expert is $500 per month."[58]

As the popular uprising against the state gradually spread throughout the country, Premier Amin reshuffled the cabinet and appointed his brother, Abdullah Amin, as chief security officer of the northern provinces, and his nephew and son-in-law, Dr. Asadullah Amin, as deputy foreign minister and director general of the intelligence service, the *Kargari Estikhbarati Muassisa* (KAM) (Workers Intelligence Institute). Premier Amin also assigned most of his relatives and loyalists to key government posts while he himself assumed the responsibility of the defense department; President Taraki remained as a figurehead.

The emergence of Premier Amin at the top commanding post within the state apparatus provided people with an opportunity to speculate on the possibility of a rift developing between President Taraki and Premier Amin. However, President Taraki consistently denied such accusations on the basis that "our enemies tell lies that there is a difference between me and Amin but I tell them that we are like flesh and nail and flesh and nail cannot be separated from each other."[59]

President Taraki visited Havana, Cuba, and on his way back to Afghanistan stopped in Moscow for consultation with the Soviet party leaders about developments in Afghanistan. President Taraki met General Secretary Leonid Brezhnev and the exiled leader of the Parcham faction of the PDPA, Barbrak Karmal, and a decision was made to unite both the Parcham and Khalq factions and send Premier Amin into diplomatic exile because they believed that it was Premier Amin who turned the people against the objectives of the April "revolution." In the meeting a decision was also made to return to the national democratic program by bringing nonparty members into the government, particularly distant members of the deposed King Zahir and other prominent figures of the previous government.[60]

While President Taraki was in Moscow his supporters Colonel Mohammad Aslam Watanjar, minister of the interior; Major Sherjan Mazdoryar, minister of frontier affairs; Colonel Sayed M. Gulabzoy, minister of communication; and Assadullah Sarwari, director of the Intelligence Service Department were planning to assassinate Premier Amin. The "gang of four's" plan was to assassinate Premier Amin while he was enroute to Kabul airport to welcome home President Taraki. Premier Amin was informed of the plot by his secret man in the Intelligence Service Department. He changed the time and the route to the airport and ordered his supporters in the army to stay alert.

To celebrate President Taraki's return to Kabul supporters and members of the PDPA forced all state employees, students, and workers to participate in a welcoming reception for President Taraki on the streets from the airport to the palace. When President Taraki's plane landed at Kabul International Airport Premier Amin greeted him and escorted him to his car. On the way to the Presidential Palace Taraki was greeted by crowds of supporters. The party members were shouting "Long live Comrade Taraki." Radio Afghanistan described the reception:

The great leader of the people of Afghanistan, Noor Mohammad Taraki, . . . today returned to the beloved country and was warmly and unprecedentedly received by noble and patriotic people, carrying flowers and revolutionary slogans. . . . After the airport ceremonies our great leader Noor Mohammad Taraki was escorted by Hafizullah Amin, . . . his faithful student and the great commander of the Great Saur "revolution," up to the side of his special car. . . . He was given a rousing and tumultuous welcome by thousands of patriotic citizens who were carrying thousands of pictures of the great leader of the people. . . . They were shouting slogans of: Good Health to Comrade Taraki.[61]

When President Taraki arrived at the People's House (Presidential Palace) he called Premier Amin to attend a dinner with him. Premier

Amin went to the palace and after an exchange of formal conversation about the country and the party, Premier Amin submitted a paper to President Taraki which contained names of the "gang of four" and requested President Taraki to dismiss them from their duties. President Taraki glanced at the paper and did not say anything. When Premier Amin was leaving the palace, President Taraki told Premier Amin that it is for the good of the country and the party if he accepts a position as ambassador abroad. Premier Amin was enraged and told him that he is the one who must resign of old age and loss of senses. Premier Amin left the palace and later that evening called President Taraki and told him that if he does not dismiss the "gang of four" he would not obey him as the president of the country. President Taraki held a meeting with the "gang of four" and a plot was designed to summon Premier Amin to the palace for lunch and murder him.

Premier Amin was informed about the plot by his secret friend Major Sayed Daoud Taroon who was President Taraki's aide-de-camp. Premier Amin insisted again on the dismissal of the "gang of four." Since the plot failed, President Taraki and the "gang of four" called Premier Amin to come to the palace on the pretense that the Soviet ambassador wanted to mediate with them in resolving their differences. Premier Amin agreed to go but arrived early to see if there was a plot so he could escape. When Premier Amin entered the palace and went to see President Taraki in his chamber, shots were fired. Premier Amin escaped, but his guards Major Taroon and Mr. Nawab Ali died on the spot.

Premier Amin went straight to the Defense Ministry and took command of the army and instructed his supporters in the army to surround the palace. President Taraki was arrested and murdered. The state-controlled radio announced that President Taraki resigned from his post because of poor health and announced his death a few days later. The "gang of four" sought refuge in the Soviet embassy compound in Kabul and were transported by the Soviet embassy to the Tadjikistan republic of the Soviet Union and remained there until the Soviet invasion of the country in December 1979. On 15 September 1979 Premier Amin officially dismissed the "gang of four" and other members of the cabinet who were loyal to President Taraki.[62]

On 16 September 1979 Premier Amin convened a meeting of the Central Committee and got himself elected as General Secretary of the PDPA and head of the state. President Amin praised Major Taroon and Mr. Nawab Ali for giving their lives for him and renamed the city of

Jalal Abad after Taroon and Lashkargah after Nawab Ali. To consolidate his power President Amin also tried to remove members of the Parcham faction of the PDPA from key administrative and military posts. He also tried to exonerate himself by proclaiming "justice, legality, and security" as his main policy program. President Amin condemned the late President Taraki and his associates as being responsible for the death of thousands of political prisoners and other innocent civilians who disappeared between April 1978 and September 1979. President Amin's pursuit of this policy did not alter the situation because people held him also responsible for the torture, murder, and disappearance of opposition leaders and innocent civilians.

To appease the people President Amin freed those prisoners who had criminal cases pending and civilians who had been randomly rounded up during antiregime rallies in towns and villages, but soon filled the prisons with opposition forces. Though the Intelligence Service Department was extensively engaged in searching houses to arrest suspected people, its activities were intensified when Amin became president and prime minister. Political suffocation and harassment became part of daily life to the extent that people were saying goodbye to members of their family and friends, not knowing whether they would be alive or not the next day. The reign of President Amin has been characterized by a U.S. diplomat in Kabul as having

An atmosphere of mortal fear and dread prevailing [in] the country, as virtually every Afghan (even some loyal Khalqis) wonders if tonight is his night to fall into the clutches of the security authorities, perhaps to disappear into one of the country's overcrowded prisons, never to [be] heard from again.[63]

In order to expand his social base of power President Amin reversed some of the state policies concerning social reforms. The new policies allowed maintaining small landownership; encouraged national capitalists; and guaranteed protection of religion.[64] President Amin also resorted to Islam to create a basis of legitimacy to his rule. To this end President Amin began repairing mosques and building new ones. He also bribed some submissive clerics to proclaim him *Olulamr* (he who rules through the authority of God).

SOVIET POLICY TOWARD AFGHANISTAN

The Soviet leadership was not pleased with events in Afghanistan, especially when Amin became General Secretary of PDPA and head of the state on 16 September 1979. The Soviet leadership did not send a congratulatory message to him until 19 September 1979. This made President Amin suspicious of the Soviet leadership and he remained cautious in his relationship with the Soviet Union. President Amin was aware that the Soviet Union had permitted his main rival, Babrak Karmal, head of the Parcham faction of the PDPA, to stay in Moscow. Even in May 1979 President Amin criticized the Soviet Union for sheltering what he called the "enemies of the working class" in the Soviet Union. President Amin also told the Soviet leadership to recall its ambassador Mr. Puzanov from Afghanistan because he considered Ambassador Puzanov to be part of the assassination conspiracy on 14 September 1979.

Although President Amin seized state and political power, he was not in a position to maintain stability because the PDPA was torn by dissension and the army by desertion. Resistance forces supported by Pakistan and the United States were gaining strength and beating the government forces. It was during this time that President Amin decided to normalize Afghanistan's relations with Pakistan. President Amin was trying to convince the leadership in Pakistan that his government was ready to recognize the Durand Line as the official border line between Afghanistan and Pakistan and cease any political and military support to the Pakistan opposition leaders in exile in Afghanistan on the condition that Pakistan should cease its support to the opposition forces operating from bases in Pakistan.

President Amin tried to arrange a meeting with the leadership in Pakistan regarding this matter. Since Pakistan received a substantial amount of U.S. aid because of developments in Afghanistan and the influx of refugees to Pakistan since the establishment of a "democratic" state in Afghanistan in April 1978, it was not prepared to engage in official dialogue with the leadership in Afghanistan unless the United States made a conciliatory move toward the Afghanistan government. This led President Amin to send signals to the United States concerning the normalization of relations between the two countries. During an interview in Kabul, President Amin told Western reporters that the government in Afghanistan wanted the United States to study the situation in Afghanistan and provide the country with more assistance.[65]

The security situation in Afghanistan was deteriorating daily. Factional fighting within the PDPA further aggravated the situation. Followers and supporters of the late President Taraki were trying to avenge him. They assassinated President Amin's nephew Asadullah Amin, deputy minister of foreign affairs and director general of the Intelligence Service Department (KAM). Since President Amin did not receive any support from the United States and Pakistan he had no other option but to rely on the Soviets. To crush the resistance forces and to maintain stability President Amin asked the Soviet Union to send a small contingent of the Red Army to Afghanistan. President Amin was of the opinion that while the Red Army protected the capital, Kabul, the government forces could fight resistance forces in the countryside. President Amin believed that by engaging the army to fight the resistance outside Kabul he would eliminate the possibility of a military coup against him by forces loyal to the late President Taraki.

Since the Soviet leadership was not happy with President Amin, they were trying to find ways and means to oust him. The Soviet leadership wanted to surrender Amin quietly and force him to resign from the leadership in favor of Babrak Karmal, head of the Parcham faction of the PDPA, with the threat that he would be put on trial for the murder of the late President Taraki. If this option failed the Soviets would use the Red Army already in Kabul to remove President Amin and install Babrak Karmal.

The Soviet leadership decided to instruct Soviet cooks in the Presidential Palace to use drugs in President Amin's food. Since President Amin did not trust Afghan nationals to work as cooks or housekeepers in the palace for fear that they might poison him, he hired several Soviets as cooks, maids, and personal physician. The Soviet cooks carried out the instruction and then left the palace shortly after the contaminated lunch was served to the president. President Amin lost consciousness and the presidential guard called upon doctors to come to the rescue. After a while Soviet and Afghan doctors came and examined President Amin. The Soviet doctor was trying to send President Amin to the Soviet Medical Corps. Since President Amin was showing signs of recuperating, the presidential guard did not transfer President Amin to the custody of the Soviets. The plot failed to ensure a peaceful surrender of President Amin, therefore the Soviets resorted to the use of its military force already in Kabul. It was early in the evening on 27 December 1979 that the Soviet troops stormed the palace and successfully eliminated President Amin and his supporters and installed Babrak Karmal as head of the state in Afghanistan.[66]

General Secretary of the Communist Party of the Soviet Union Leonid Brezhnev during an interview justified sending troops to Afghanistan on the grounds that

the unceasing armed intervention, the well advanced plot by external forces of reaction created a real threat that Afghanistan would lose its independence and be turned into an imperialist military bridgehead on our country's southern border. In other words, the time came when we no longer could but respond to the request of the government of friendly Afghanistan. To have acted otherwise would have meant leaving Afghanistan a prey to imperialism, allowing the aggressive forces to repeat in that country what they had succeeded in doing, for instance, in Chile where the peoples freedom was drowned in blood. To act otherwise would have meant to watch passively the origination on our southern border of a seat of serious danger to the security of the Soviet state.[67]

The Soviet Union's main concern, however, was to defend its interests and to project itself as a power in the region. The Soviet policy of moving troops into Afghanistan has been stated by a senior political columnist in *Izvestia:*

We knew that the decision to bring in troops would not be popular in the modern world, even if it was absolutely legal. But we also knew that we would have ceased to be a great power if we refrained from carrying the burden of taking unpopular but necessary decisions, extraordinary decisions prompted by extraordinary circumstances.[68]

NOTES

1. Text of the speech by President Mohammad Daoud via Radio Afghanistan, *Afghanistan* 24 (September 1973):3.

2. Afghanistan, Ministry of Planning, *Democratic Republic of Afghanistan's Annual 1979* (Kabul: Government Printing House, 1979), p. 380.

3. Louis Dupree, "A Note on Afghanistan: 1974," *AUFS Reports* 18 (September 1974):7–8.

4. Afghanistan, *Afghanistan's Republic Annual 1975* (Kabul: The Kabul Times Publishing Agency, 1975), p. 246.

5. *The Quarterly Economic Review: Pakistan, Bangladesh, Afghanistan* (London: The Economist Intelligence Unit 1975), no. 3, p. 17.

6. *The Kabul Times*, 12 November 1974.

7. Vladimir Glukhoded, "Economy of Independent Afghanistan," in *Afghanistan: Past and Present* (Moscow: USSR. Academy of Sciences, Oriental Studies in the U.S.S.R., no. 3, 1981), p. 234.

8. Akhgar (Sazmani Mubariza Bara-e-Azadi Tabaqa-e-Kargar or Organization for Liberation of Working Class), *Afghanistan* (Tehran 1980), p. 99.

9. *Afghanistan Council Newsletter* 7 (June 1979), p. 5.

10. Afghanistan, *Democratic Republic of Afghanistan's Annual 1979*, op. cit., p. 1,426.

11. Louis Dupree, "Toward Representative Government in Afghanistan," *AUFS Reports* 14 (1978):2.

12. *The Quarterly Economic Review of Pakistan, Bangladesh, Afghanistan*, 1977, op. cit., p. 37; 1975, p. 19.

13. Irwin Silber, *Afghanistan—The Battle Line is Drawn* (San Francisco: Line of March Publications, 1980), p. 23.

14. Thomas T. Hammond, *Red Flag Over Afghanistan* (Boulder: Westview Press, 1984), p. 38.

15. G. S. Bhargava, *South Asian Security After Afghanistan* (Washington, DC: Lexington Books, 1983), p. 34.

16. *The Quarterly Economic Review*, 1974, op. cit., no. 3, p. 20.

17. *The Quarterly Economic Review*, 1975, op. cit., no. 3, p. 20.

18. Afghanistan, *Afghanistan Republic's Annual 1975*, op. cit., p. 222.

19. *The Quarterly Economic Review*, 1976, op. cit., p. 18.

20. Ibid., p. 20.

21. Quoted from Tahir Amin, *Afghanistan in Crisis* (Islamabad: Institute of Policy Studies, 1982), p. 71.

22. *The Statesman*, (New Delhi), 22 June 1947.

23. Afghanistan, *Afghanistan Republic's Annual*, 1976, op. cit., p. 25.

24. Tariq Ali, *Can Pakistan Survive: The Death of a State* (New York: Pelican Books, 1983), p. 71.

25. Afghanistan, *Afghanistan Republic's Annual 1976*, op. cit., p. 91.

26. Afghanistan, *Afghanistan Republic's Annual 1975*, op. cit., pp. 71–72.

27. Louis Dupree, "Afghanistan 1977: Does Trade Plus Aid Guarantee Development?" *AUFS Reports* 21 (August 1977):2.

28. *The Quarterly Economic Review*, 1975, op. cit., p. 21.

29. Ibid., no. 1, p. 16.

30. *The Quarterly Economic Review*, 1976, op. cit., p. 20.

31. *The Documents from the US Espionage Den*, Section (1) Afghanistan, By Muslim Students Following The Line of the Imam (Tehran: Entisharati Azadi, n.d.), pp. 43–48.

32. Ibid., p. 43.

33. Ibid., p. 50.

34. *The Quarterly Economic Review*, 1977, op. cit., p. 20.

35. *Wall Street Journal*, 2 September 1977.

36. U.S., US Agency for International Development, *Helping People* (Kabul: United States Embassy, April 1976), p. 35; *The Quarterly Economic Review*, 1975, p. 21; 1976, p. 18; 1977, p. 17.

37. *The Documents from the US Espionage Den*, op. cit., p. 47.

38. Akhgar., op. cit., p. 49.

39. Hamidullah Amin and Gordon B. Schilz, *A Geography of Afghanistan* (Kabul: Kabul University and Center For Afghanistan Studies at the Univeristy of Nebraska-Omaha, 1976), p. 170.

40. *Resolution of the PDPA Students Association*, Kabul, 1976.

41. Anthony Arnold, *Afghanistan: The Soviet Invasion in Perspective* (California: Hoover Institution Press, 1981), p. 65.

42. Henry S. Bradsher, *Afghanistan and the Soviet Union* (Durham: Duke University Press, 1985), p. 66.

43. Ibid., p. 69.

44. General Union of Democratic Students and Patriotic Afghans (GUDSPA), *Pasikh ba Sazmani Fidayian-e-Mujahidini Karaj dar Iran* [A response to the Fidayian-e-Mujahid organization of Karaj in Iran], pp. 4–5.

45. Noor Mohammad Taraki, "The Basic Lines of Revolutionary Duties of the Democratic Republic of Afghanistan," *Democratic Republic of Afghanistan's Annual* 7 Saur 1358 (Kabul: The Kabul Times Publishing Agency, April 1979), pp. 62–70.

46. Afghanistan, *Democratic Republic of Afghanistan's Annual 1979*, op. cit., p. 125.

47. Text of speech by Noor Mohammad Taraki, *Afghanistan* 32 (June 1979):1.

48. Text of speech by Hafizullah Amin, *Afghanistan* 32 (June 1979):24–28.

49. Ibid.

50. Afghanistan, *Democratic Republic of Afghanistan's Annual 1979*, op. cit., p. 708.

51. Ibid., pp. 131–36.

52. *Amnesty International Report*. (London: Amnesty International Publications, 1980), p. 176.

53. General Union of Democratic Students and Patriotic Afghans (GUDSPA) op. cit., pp. 6–9.

54. Afghanistan, *Democratic Republic of Afghanistan's Annual 1979*, op. cit., p. 258.

55. Amnesty International, op. cit., 1980, p. 177.

56. Afghanistan, *Democratic Republic of Afghanistan's Annual 1979*, op. cit., p. 356.

57. John Scherer, *USSR Facts and Figures Annual* (Gulf Breeze: Academic International Press, 1987), vol. 2, p. 259.

58. Afghanistan, *Democratic Republic of Afghanistan's Annual 1979*, op. cit., p. 332.

59. Ibid., p. 333.

60. Alexandre Dastarac and M. Levant, "What Went Wrong in Afghanistan," *Merip Reports* 89 (July-August 1980):6.

61. Broadcast by Radio Afghanistan in English, 11 September 1979, Foreign Broadcast Information Service (hereafter credited as FBIS), *Middle East and North African Series*, 12 September 1979, pp. 3–4.

62. *The Kabul Times*, 15 September 1979, p. 1.

63. Cable no. 8073 from Kabul to Department of State, 20 November 1979, pp. 6–7.

64. Alexandre Dastarac and M. Levant, op. cit., p. 8.

65. *The Kabul Times*, 28 October 1979.

66. Raja Anwar, *The Tragedy of Afghanistan* (New York and London: Verso, 1988), pp. 183–93.

67. Neues Deutschland, *About Events in Afghanistan: The Answers of Leonid Brezhnev, General Secretary of the Central Committee of the CPSU to Questions put to Him by a Correspondent of Pravda on 13 January 1980*, German Democratic Republic, 15 January 1980, pp. 5–6.

68. Cited in J. Steel, *World Powers: Soviet Foreign Policy Under Brezhnev And Andropov* (London: Michael Joseph, 1983), p. 116.

4 Politics of the Resistance

ISLAMIC MOVEMENT

The Islamic empire established its domination over territories in Western and Central Asian regions as early as seventh century AD. At the early stage of its expansion and consolidation Islam did not seek to convert the dominated people to the Islamic faith but subjected the "protected people of the book" to pay taxes to the Muslims. Gradual conversion into Islam began much later in order to (a) reduce the burden of taxation and (b) to maintain class domination and social positions by having people identify themselves with the religion of the rulers. The early converts to Islam were feudal landowners. They accepted Islam in order to be able to reduce their taxes and maintain their positions. The number of people who wished to be converted to Islam continuously increased to the extent that the revenue from tax collection declined year by year. This forced the Islamic empire to order the converts to pay the same amount of taxes as they paid prior to their conversion into Islam.

In spite of the theoretical equality of believers, Islam did not change the fabric of the socioeconomic structure in its territories. On the contrary, it strengthened the (economic) differences between rich and poor by encouraging the latter to obey the former. According to the Holy Quran

[W]e portion out among them their livelihood in the life of this world, and we exalt some of them above others in rank, that some of them may take others in service. And the mercy of thy Lord is better than that which they amass.[1] Allah had made some of you excel others in the means of subsistence; so those who are made to excel give not away their sustenance to those whom their right hands possess, so that they may be equal therein.[2]

By embracing Islam feudal landowners maintained their socioeconomic privileges as before.

Historical Background

Those in leadership positions in Afghanistan after the country's independence in 1919 initiated socioeconomic reforms aimed at building a civil society where religion would be separate from politics and the state. For this reason they tried to use the state to limit the power of feudal landowners, some of whom were also in charge of religious affairs in various parts of the country. Feudal landowners and religious leaders, having lost their privilege were quick to aspire to regain their positions. Thus they rebelled against the state, backed by their peasant supporters and followers, claiming that the state violated Islam. They called for a "Jihad" as a necessary means to restore Islamic traditions. The collapse of the state in 1929 was the result of opposition by feudal landowners and religious clerics. Since then Islam has remained a state religion. The ruling classes resorted to Islam and promoted it in order to legitimize their rule and their class domination. They used religion not only to shield themselves against a delegitimation crisis but also to keep the illiterate and rebellious peasantry under their control.

The ruling class, since the downfall of the state under the leadership of King Amanullah in 1929, has not been able to improve the impoverished conditions of the majority of the people in Afghanistan. The plight of the peasantry and blue-collar work forces, on the one hand, and the failure of the state to provide employment opportunities for the educated social strata (intellectuals advocating socialist development strategies) graduating from technical schools and other institutes of higher education in the 1960s, on the other, caused the ruling class to regard the formation of an Islamic movement as a counterbalance to the spreading influence of radical discourse among intellectuals, students, workers, and other disenchanted social strata. There was no Islamic organization as such in the early 1960s but the spread of Islamic views developed around publication of newspapers or periodicals such as *Mardum* (People) in 1966 and the religious-oriented newspapers *Gahiz* (Morning), *Nida-e-Haq* (Voice of Truth), and *Afkar-e-Naw* (New Thought) through which people could express their religious views. The further spread of Islamic agitation finally culminated in the formation of the Islamic movement in 1969 as an alternative political movement to reduce the influence of the revolutionary and communist activities in Afghanistan.[3]

A number of professors of Islamic studies at Kabul University who advocated an Islamic way of life organized the religious group of Sazmani Jawanani Musulman known as Eikhwan-ul-Muslimin. Members of the group began enlisting supporters from among the students of Kabul University and developed into a political organization known as *Jamiat-e-Islami-e-Afghanistan* (the Islamic Society of Afghanistan). Prominent leaders active in the formation of the organization were Ghulam Mohammad Niazi, president, Abdul Rab Rasoul Sayaf, and Sayed Mohammad Musa Tawana. After the death of Niazi, Burhanuddin Rabbani was elected president of the organization. The power struggle within the organization soon led to a split. A new group emerged in 1969 under the leadership of Gulbuddin Hikmatyar, a student at the College of Engineering at Kabul University.

The prime objective of the Islamic movement was to press the leadership to Islamicize the state apparatus. Members of the movement objected to the modernization trend in the country and decried women's freedom and emancipation as anti-Islam. During a women's protest demonstration in Kabul a Mullah threw acid on women, seriously wounding them. When he was arrested he said he would do it again if he was released.[4] To propagate Islamic ideology, members of the Islamic movement not only held meetings and rallies but also organized action groups to fight opponents of the Islamic movement in the country. For instance, during a meeting at Kabul University in June 1973 supporters of Eikhwan-ul-Muslimin launched an offense on supporters of the New Democratic Organization (*Shula-e-Jawid*). This resulted in the death of Saidal Sukhandan, a prominent ideologue of the organization, and the injury of numerous others.[5]

Shortly after this incident the editor of *Gahiz,* a weekly Islamic paper, was murdered at his home. Many believed that members of the New Democratic Organization committed this act in revenge for the death of Saidal. *Jamiat-e-Islami* (Islamic Society) blamed the Soviets for the murder of Saidal, arguing that by murdering Saidal the Soviets saw the opportunity to incite both the Islamic groups and supporters of the New Democratic Organization to fight each other. When Mohammad Daoud seized political power in July 1973 and proclaimed Afghanistan a republic, he banned political parties and imprisoned and executed key opposition leaders. This led leaders of the New Democratic Organization to go underground while the leaders of the Islamic organizations such as Hikmatyar and Rabbani and others fled to Pakistan.

Islamic fundamentalists, liberal and conservative social forces regarded President Daoud's socialist-oriented policy as a threat to their interests and decided to fight him. It was during the first year of Daoud's rule that supporters of Hikmatyar, in collaboration with feudal landowners and pro-Western social forces attacked various state-owned installations in Panjshir, Herat, and Laghman provinces. The Islamic forces were not in a position to overthrow the state in Kabul; their main goal was to warn President Daoud that such antistate activities would continue if he did not abandon his socialist rhetoric and abide by Islamic traditions.[6]

Rabbani and Hikmatyar along with some of their supporters languished in Pakistan during the five years of President Daoud's rule (1973–1978). They failed to bridge their ideological differences to form a unified party. Following the overthrow of President Daoud and the establishment of a "democratic" state headed by Noor Mohammad Taraki in 1978, Hikmatyar formed his own party known as *Hizbi Islami-e-Afghanistan* (the Islamic Party of Afghanistan).

Post-1978 Islamic Movement

When the spontaneous uprising of the people against the "democratic" state in Kabul started, some of the supporters of the Islamic organizations in association with local religious clerics not only engaged in antistate agitation but also directed their attack against state employees, teachers, and students on the pretext that they were communist agents. They protested the repression practiced by the pro-Soviet People's Democratic Party of Afghanistan (PDPA), equating it with communism. They murdered and tortured many innocent civilians. In Herat province several teachers, government officials, and military officers who had no ties with the ruling party in Afghanistan were killed.[7]

Prior to the emergence of the "democratic" state in April 1978, both the Jamiat-e-Islami and Hizbi Islami lacked substantial organizational structures. Following the post-1978 political changes in Afghanistan they managed to consolidate themselves and improve their organization with funds from the United States and other Western countries.[8] The socioeconomic reforms introduced by the "democratic" state antagonized feudal landowners, some of the industrial and merchant bourgeoisie as well as the comprador bourgeoisie. Since they did not have a political party of their own, they supported the Pakistan-based Islamic parties.

The spontaneous uprisings of landowners, businessmen, peasants, and intellectuals against the "democratic" state began with various motivations. There was not a nationally based organization to unite and lead them in their struggle against the state in Kabul. This situation provided an opportunity for Islamic parties who had already established themselves in Pakistan to use religion as a unifying force in the resistance against the regime in Kabul. As the uprising continued throughout the country and the state intensified its efforts to eliminate opposition leaders, more religious clerics left the country to settle in Pakistan and begin organizing their supporters.

The numbers of Islamic parties mushroomed in Peshawar, Pakistan. Accordingly there are numerous parties, but the ones recognized by the West are the following:

1. *Hizbi Islami* (Islamic Party) headed by Gulbuddin Hikmatyar.

2. *Hizbi Islami* (Islamic Party) headed by Mohammad Yunus Khalis. This splintered faction of Hikmatyar's Islamic Party (and with the same name) is a relatively small group and operates mainly in Nangarhar and Paktiya provinces.

3. *Jamiat-e-Islami* (Islamic Society) headed by Burhanuddin Rabbani.

4. *Mahazi Islami* (National Islamic Front) headed by Sayed Ahmad Gaillani.

5. *Jabha-e-Milli-e-Nijat* (National Liberation Front) headed by Sebghatullah Mujaddadi.

6. *Harakat-i-Enqilab-i-Islami* (Islamic Revolutionary Movement) headed by Mohammad Nabi Mohammadi.

7. *Itihadi Islami Baraye Azadi Afghanistan* (Islamic Union for Liberation of Afghanistan) headed by Abdul Rab Rasoul Sayaf.[9]

While these and other Pakistan-based Islamic parties maintained their independent organizational structures, ideologically they can be classified into two main groups: (a) the fundamentalists and (b) the moderates.

The fundamentalists are comprised of the Islamic Party by Hikmatyar, the Islamic Society by Rabbani, and the Islamic Party by Khalis. The group is known as the Islamic Unity of Afghanistan Mujahidin. The main ideological thrust of the camp is Islamic fundamentalism and the establishment of an Islamic state in Afghanistan. Gulbuddin Hikmatyar, head of the Islamic Party, told a Dutch reporter during an interview that

democracy and Islam do not go together; that is a very un-Islamic state. Afghanistan will be a strict Islamic state. A group of wise men will adapt the laws to Islam. . . . All alcohol will be banned, women will stay at home once again, and the mullahs will have more power.[10]

The Islamic Society of Rabbani stated its position as follows:

Establishment of [an] Islamic system forms our main obligation and our sacred aim. . . . Jamiat wants to improve relations between the owner of the land and farmer, employer and employee in such a way that instead of fighting against each other they live in a cooperative atmosphere.[11]

The moderates which are comprised of the industrial bourgeoisie, liberals, former bureaucrats, feudal landowners, and traditional religious leaders, are known as the Islamic Alliance of the Mujahidin of Afghanistan. Since the government in Kabul also promotes Islam, repairs mosques and builds new ones in order to win the support of the people and neutralize the campaign of the Pakistan-based Islamic parties, the moderates are forced to concentrate on issues such as human rights, freedom of speech, of assembly, etc., that people have been denied in Afghanistan since the establishment of the "democratic" state in April 1978.

Sayed Ahmad Gaillani, Sebghatullah Mujaddadi, and Mohammad Nabi Mohammadi are the leading personalities of the camp that supports the return of deposed King Zahir as a symbol of unity. Most leaders of the camp come from upper class backgrounds. For instance, Gaillani was an urban businessman who until the Soviet invasion of the country on 27 December 1979 was the proprietor of the Peugeot automobile dealership in Kabul. He is respected by a large section of Pushtun tribes in the country.

His family's inter-marriage with the ruling Kabul elites, his personal wealth, and generally Western orientation have earned him a reputation that attracts former bureaucrats to his side, makes him more acceptable to the United States, and in the opinion of some, renders him a better candidate to compromise with the Soviet government on the restoration of an independent Afghanistan. . . . Gaillani apparently views the former monarch as capable of attracting segments of the peasantry within the country, the refugees and moderate Islamic countries to his Islamic alliance camp.[12]

These Islamic parties lacked a well-articulated socioeconomic policy as an alternate to the development strategy in Afghanistan and offered no solution to the question of land distribution, national oppression and, in particular, women's liberation. The women's movement and its participation in Afghanistan politics began following World War II and the number of women employees in various socioeconomic developmental projects increased in the 1960s and 1970s. During the constitutional period (1963-1973) women from upper and middle class backgrounds participated in the state bureaucracy as ministers and parliamentarians. Women were employed in the army as well as in the police departments in Kabul. It was during this period that women of upper and middle class families discarded the veil and began to fight for their rights in the male-dominated society of Afghanistan. The movement was in its embryonic stage, but it is considered to have been a step forward toward women's emancipation at that stage of the country's development. Today the Islamic parties reinforce wearing of the veil and Islamic dress for women and do not let them take part in the resistance, outdoor activities, or work in the milieu of men.

In addition to the Pakistan-based Islamic parties there are several other Islamic organizations which are based in Iran. Some of the Iran-based Islamic organizations enjoy political, economic, and military support of the religious leadership in Iran. According to a French reporter,

the Iranians consider the Soviet invasion of Afghanistan the most favorable situation for the consolidation and extension of their influence in the country. In the beginning they decided to help all the Hazara groups without discrimination. When it did not work according to their wishes, they changed their policy and decided to federate the groups under the umbrella of one organization, Nasr, a party which they found the best organized. Nasr, founded in 1980, is the amalgamation of two parties. . . . But last year [1982] the Iranians sent a delegation to Hazarajat in order to investigate the activities of Nasr and to see how their military and financial help was being used. The Iranians were deeply disappointed and convinced that it was impossible to accomplish anything with the Afghan parties. Then they decided to operate through their own Iranian party inside Afghanistan and created the Sepah-e-Pasdaran; it has the same structure and the same organization as the Iranian Islamic Revolutionary Party, only the members are Afghans.[13]

The popularity of Ayatollah Khomeini among the Shiite population of Afghanistan has been described by a French newsman as such that "in Hazarajat, the portrait of Khomeini is part of the decor. The people display it ostentatiously everywhere, over the doorways of their huts and in the bazaars, in the inns and public buildings."[14] The Iran-based Islamic organizations are antimonarchy in their philosophical and political orientations, opposed to King Zahir and his exiled bureaucrats for assuming the leadership of the national liberation war in Afghanistan, and regard the Islamic parties based in Peshawar, Pakistan, as pro-Western parties. These organizations remain loyal to the political philosophy of the Ayatollah and follow the Ayatollah's famous dictum—neither East nor West but Islam. There are 20 or more such organizations but the well-organized ones are the following:

1. *Al-Nasr* Organization (Victory) headed by Mir Hoseyn Sadequi.
2. *Shura-e-Itifaki Islami* (Council of Islamic Unity) headed by Ayatollah Bihishti from Bamiyan province of Afghanistan.
3. *Raad* (Thunder) headed by Shaikhzada Khazaei.
4. *Hizbullah* (the Party of God) headed by Shaikh Ali Wusuki.[15]

The Pakistan-based Islamic parties enjoy the ideological, political, and economic support of the government of Pakistan and that of the Persian Gulf states. It is for this reason that the Pakistan-based Islamic parties maintain cordial relationships with the leadership in Pakistan and the Arab countries in the Middle East. They regard the issue of Pushtunistan (a long-disputed issue between the ruling classes of both countries, Afghanistan and Pakistan) as a Soviet fabrication aimed at dividing Islamic countries in the region. The Iran-based Islamic organizations remain silent on this question but condemn the Pakistan-based Islamic parties as an ally of Western imperialism. They defend Iran in its war against Iraq and actively participate in that war to defend the Islamic Republic of Iran.

The Pakistan- and Iran-based Islamic parties are divided not only along a philosophical line but also by tribal loyalties. Most leaders of the Islamic parties (either in Pakistan or Iran) come from big landowning families and prior to the Soviet invasion were in charge of religious affairs in their respective districts. During the nine years of war, leaders of the Islamic parties have failed to narrow personal and tribal cleavages that exist among them or to coordinate their activities. Many instances have been recorded when these Islamic parties, associated with one or the other feudal landowners, assaulted and disarmed one another. For instance, a copy of a secret document of the *Hizbi Islami* (under the leadership of Hikmatyar) was revealed and published in the *Independent Afghanistan:*

Members of the Hizbi Islami while fighting against the "Red Satan" must corner, isolate, and even eliminate the other rebel groups in order to project the image of Hizbi Islami-e-Afghanistan. If you consider yourselves weaker militarily to act against them [other groups of the alliance] then the Commander can inform the occupant Russians or their dependents about domiciles of alien guerrillas.[16]

These Islamic parties not only fight one another but also exact heavy tribute from members of their rival parties and organizations who cross the area of their control as well as from local people in the countryside.

THE REVOLUTIONARY MOVEMENT

Historical Background

The roots of the revolutionary movements can be traced back to early student movements in the 1960s. The struggle for a new democratic society in Afghanistan accelerated largely because of economic hardship and the example of national liberation movements elsewhere. Excessive poverty, high unemployment, and political repression forced many people to embrace a radical antiestablishment discourse and to agitate the blue-collar workers and peasants in hopes of enlisting them in the cause of a new democratic revolution. Meanwhile, national liberation movements in the colonies and semi-colonies in Asia, Africa, and Latin American countries spurred people in Afghanistan to fight for their democratic rights and liberties.

These internal and external factors forced the ruling class to liberalize state policies and allow the formation of political organizations. Intellectuals who advocated a revolutionary transformation of the country organized themselves and formed the New Democratic Organization of Afghanistan known as *Shula-e- Jawid* (Eternal Flame) in 1964. Because of its espousal of ''revolutionary'' armed struggle and its radical discourse, it attracted a large number of intellectuals in cities and villages throughout the country as well as students in Afghanistan's universities and high schools. The organization served as a mother organization of the leftist movement in organizing many professional revolutionaries in Afghanistan. The prominent founding figures of the organization were Dr. Hadi Mahmoodi, Professor Akram Yari, and Mohammad Usman.[17]

Shula-e-Jawid was also the name of the theoretical and political organ of the organization. The organization supported the rights to self-determination of nations and encouraged support for one inside Afghanistan should such a struggle ever arise. It is for this reason that the organization earned the overwhelming support of the oppressed people in the country. The organization condemned the nonviolent and ''evolutionary'' transition to socialism and supported armed struggle inside and outside the country. The organization also supported the ideological and political line of the Communist Party of China concerning national and international questions.

The New Democratic Organization engaged in intensive ideological, political, and organizational work not only among students but also among industrial workers. The organization was responsible for more than 14 students and workers strikes and rallies throughout the country in the late 1960s. During a protest demonstration staged by the workers and staff of the Jangalak Automotive Maintenance Repair Workshop in June 1968, police arrested more than 20 members of the organization, fined and sentenced them on accounts of antistate activities. Soon, however, the organization split into factions. There were differences over how to analyze the situation of the country. The organization could never rise to the level of a party and offer a policy program. Lacking this, the organization could not effectively combine legal and illegal methods of struggle and ended up engaging in nothing more than political adventurism.[18]

Post-1978 Revolutionary Movement

The split in the rank and file of the International Communist Movement and changes in the leadership of the Communist Party of China exacerbated the disintegration of the New Democratic Organization. There are several splintered organizations such as Paykar, Khurasan, Sazmani Watanparastani Wakiei (Sawo), etc.; the most important and well-organized ones that are active participants in the armed struggle in Afghanistan are:

1. *Sazmani Rahaye Bakhshi Khalqa-e-Afghanistan* or *Surkha* (Organization for Liberation of the People of Afghanistan)

2. *Sazmani Azadi Bakhshi Mardumi Afghanistan* or SAMA (People's Liberation Organization of Afghanistan) previously known as the Revolutionary Group of Afghanistan

3. *Akhgar* (*Sazmani Mubariza Bara-e-Azadi Tabaqa-e-Kargar* or Organization for Liberation of Working Class)

The first of these groups—*Surkha* (Organization for Liberation of the People of Afghanistan)—broke off from the New Democratic Organization sometime in the 1970s on the grounds that the New Democratic Organization had concentrated its efforts largely in overt political and ideological work among students, intellectuals, and workers in factories but failed to establish links with the masses in the countryside. Influenced by the Cultural Revolution in China, this group split from the New Democratic Organization in order to establish close links with the peasants and laborers in villages and to reeducate its rank and file by working and living among the peasant population. Surkha, later known as Rahaye, kept its revolutionary rhetoric and adheres to the theoretical discourse of the Three World Theory developed by the Communist Party of China. Despite heavy losses of its members and cadres both prior to and after the Soviet invasion, the organization continues to operate in different parts of the country against the Soviets and the state in Kabul.

The second faction listed above—SAMA (People's Liberation Organization of Afghanistan)—is generally considered to be the PLO of Afghanistan. It actually was formed in 1978 as an offshoot of the Revolutionary Group of Afghanistan (RG). When the Revolutionary Group adopted the line of the Three World Theory, Abdul Majid Kalakani and his friends left and formed their own organization, the SAMA. SAMA's point of departure from the RG is that the latter adopted a dogmatic analysis of the world situation and the revolutionary movements in Afghanistan. SAMA was founded on the basis of the necessity for an underground revolutionary organization. SAMA's program was formulated by Kalakani and his supporters and emphasizes (a) the formation of a working-class party, (b) the formation of a united front, and (c) the formation of a people's army.[19] Other organizations argued that SAMA did not pay much attention to ideological struggle and work among the people in the past and was deeply engaged in practical activities. It is for this reason that the organization bore the brunt of the charge of ''adventurism'' in the revolutionary movement in the country.

Kalakani, founder of the organization, was captured on 27 February 1980 in Kabul and was covertly executed by the government on 8 June 1980.[20] SAMA issued a statement that if Kalakani did not receive a fair trial it would retaliate. A week later, SAMA dealt a heavy blow to two army garrisons in Kabul and Shamali in Parwan province in retaliation for Kalakani's execution. Radio Afghanistan justified Kalakani's execution by calling him a ''bandit.'' News media in India and Western countries reported his execution while calling Kalakani an Afghan ''Robin Hood.''[21] The organization is active in Shamali, Ghazni, Farah, and a few other provinces. SAMA believes that its main source of power comes from the people and its munitions are manufactured in Soviet factories. After Kalakani's execution the organization split into two factions—the right and left. The right-wing faction allied with the liberal Islamic parties based in Pakistan while the left-wing faction adhered to the radical discourse of revolutionary armed struggle and maintained its antisuperpower position.

The *Akhgar* (Organization for Liberation of Working Class), was founded in 1976. The organization's main concern was to build a working class party in Afghanistan. Akhgar postulates that without a revolutionary party any revolutionary movement is bound to failure. Thus the concept of building a party was a critical point in its departure from other organizations. Akhgar addresses the Soviet Union and China as two "social-imperialist" and "revisionist" countries. Following the death of Chairman Mao Tse-tung of the Communist Party of China, the organization denounced Mao Tse-tung's thought to be anti-Marxist in its basic philosophical orientation. Later in 1982, the organization revised its stance vis-à-vis Mao Tse-tung and called him a great revolutionary leader in China but not a great Marxist-Leninist. The organization attributes both the success and the failure of the Chinese revolution to Chairman Mao. Members of the organization are active in Kabul, Herat, Kandahar, Bamiyan, and other provinces.

Akhgar believes in self-reliance and protracted armed struggle of the people and relies on internal resources in its "anti-imperialist" struggle. It treats the United States and the Soviet Union as two "imperialist" superpowers and rejects the pragmatic philosophy of playing one superpower against the other, whereas Sazmani Rahaye maintains the policy of utilizing the "inter-imperialist" contradictions and claims that forging an alliance with one superpower against the other helps the "revolutionary" movements in peripheral social formations in general, and in Afghanistan in particular.

Based on this theoretical perspective, Rahaye and the right-wing of SAMA supported the establishment of an Islamic Republican State in Afghanistan on the grounds that such a state is compatible with the general aspiration of the people as well as with political developments in the international arena. Thus, both *Rahaye* and SAMA proposed an alliance with all opposition parties to fight the Soviet forces in Afghanistan. The outcome of this proposal was the formation of *Jabha-e-Muttahid-e-Milli* (United National Front) in June 1980. Akhgar opposed such an alliance on the grounds that it places the "revolutionary" organizations at the mercy of the Islamic parties based in Pakistan. During an offensive on an army garrison at Bala Hisar, Kabul, in June 1980, jointly carried out by Rahaye and Hizbi Islami of Gulbuddin Hikmatyar,[22] Rahaye suffered heavy losses while the Islamic Party gained tremendous publicity as being the only party that carried out the operation with limited casualties. As a result the Rahaye's top leadership was severely criticized by its members.

The revolutionary organizations each have their own socioeconomic program as an alternative strategy for social development to those of the government in Afghanistan. The socioeconomic and political program articulated by the Akhgar organization is considered to be a progressive strategy in comparison to others at the present stage of development in the country. Some of the most important points of Akhgar's program are the following:

1. the establishment of a People's Democratic Republic through direct, secret and universal suffrage;

2. the establishment of a People's Council based on free election;

3. introduction of a national-progressive constitution by the General Council of the people of Afghanistan—a constitution which determines the rights and duties of state officials and citizens of the country;

4. empowerment of the people to recall their representative any time and send a new representative to the People's Council;

5. destroying the foundations of the present state apparatus (the army, the police, Intelligence Service, etc.); arming the people and creating a revolutionary army in the service of the people;

6. safeguarding the rights of individuals, property, profession, as well as the right of every citizen of the country to travel freely and to reside in whatever part of the country he/she wants to;

7. guaranteeing freedom of speech, of press, of religion, of assembly, of organizing political parties, of demonstrations, etc.;

8. supporting women's emancipation and their complete equality with man in every walk of life;

9. abrogating all individual and class privileges;

10. supporting the right to self-determination of nations even to complete secession and the establishment of a nation-state that represents all nationalities of the country and accords equal status to them;

11. abrogation of the tradition of conducting secret diplomacy and the empowerment of the people in supervising the country's foreign policy;

12. abrogation of all economic contracts with the Soviet Union and other imperial powers;

13. supporting heavy industrialization of the country for the purpose of building an independent nation;

14. maintaining the separation of religion and state, politics, education, and the recognition of religious freedom;

15. supporting free and compulsory education at the intermediate level and providing food, cloth, books, etc., free of charge to the children of the disadvantaged classes;

16. elimination of compulsory language and struggle against any manifestation of racial, cultural, and language discrimination;

17. building hospitals, residential houses, and recreational facilities, construct-
ing roads, providing drinking water, preventive medicine, insurance, etc.,
to the people and providing housing to laborers and workers free of charge.[23]

In addition to these revolutionary organizations there is another organization known by the name of *Afghan Millat* (the Social Democratic
Party of Afghanistan). Afghan Millat was founded in 1966 by members
of the royal family with participation of several bureaucrats like Sardar
Atiq, Sardar Rafiq, Hashim Mojaddadi, Abdullah Wardak, and Engineer
Ghulam Mohammad Farhad.[24] The organization's main political theme
is "Greater Afghanistan" and claims parts of Iran and Delhi of India
as historical borders of Afghanistan during the time of King Ahmad
Shah Abdali in 1747. The party was accused of being a "fascist" party
by patriotic forces and progressive organizations, and many other individual strata. The party did not articulate a radical political change
and social revolution but was for political reform within the state apparatus. It was due to this as well as myopic Pushtun nationalism that
it gained support among some intellectuals of the Pushtun nationality
in Kabul University.

The organization supported the constitution and the monarchy and
agitated the development of national economy, culture, and the promotion of the Pushtu language as the popular language in Afghanistan.
For this reason it opposed foreign films dubbed in Persian by Iranian
film industries saying, "Why don't they leave the English in? Who
understands Iranian Persian?"[25] The organization favored the prohibi-
tion of foreign luxury imports and the introduction of a progressive
income tax to support the development of a national project. The party
remained a staunch supporter of Pushtunistan and believed in the unity
of Pushtuns on both sides of the Durand Line, arguing that "water
cannot be divided with a stick." The organization participated in the
annual commemoration of the state-sponsored Pushtunistan Day in Kabul.

Despite its political rhetoric of building a strong Afghanistan, the
party failed to gain much support because the party neither articulated
the interests of the peasantry and blue-collar workers nor did it support
their struggle for socioeconomic reforms. The leaders of the party are
now either in Western countries or in Pakistan. Their role in the national
liberation struggle is insignificant. In contrast to this, the revolutionary
organizations have their bases inside the country and are better organized
in their armed struggle against the state in Afghanistan.

U.S. DIPLOMATIC POLICY TOWARD AFGHANISTAN

When Afghanistan was declared a "democratic" republic in April 1978 the United States had no choice but to recognize the regime and to maintain a "watchful waiting" attitude toward developments in the country. The Department of State instructed its embassy in Kabul that

one option would be for us to phase out our activities in Afghanistan, but we believe this would be very unsettling to Afghanistan's neighbors and incompatible with their policies. The DRA has not asked us to pack our bags and leave but on the contrary has accepted our policy of maintaining our interest and presence. Closing out our efforts in Afghanistan would likely be seen as an abdication of our responsibility and would accomplish for the Soviets one of their primary objectives, namely to reduce further U.S. and Western influence in Afghanistan and the region. It would not be in our interest to give such a blank check signed to Moscow.[26]

As spontaneous mass uprisings against the state in Afghanistan were escalating day by day the United States began supporting and reorganizing Islamic fundamentalists who were in exile in Pakistan and providing them with financial and military assistance to fight the "democratic" regime in Kabul.[27] The United States appointed Adolph Dubs as a new ambassador to Afghanistan with the hope that the new ambassador would be able to support oppositions forces in Kabul. Ambassador Dubs was kidnapped in Kabul on 14 February 1979 by four armed men whom the regime in Kabul claimed to be members of Sitami Milli Organization demanding the release of their leaders Mr. Tahir Badakhshi and Bahruddin Bais and others from prisons in Afghanistan. During the rescue mission carried out by the state under the supervision of Soviet advisors, Ambassador Dubs was killed. The U.S. government protested against the methods employed in the rescue mission and particularly the presence of Soviet advisors and their direction of the operation.[28]

Following the death of Ambassador Dubs, the U.S.-Afghanistan relationship declined and the White House announced a severe reduction in its assistance programs in Afghanistan which were projected for 1979 and 1980 and terminated its military assistance program that was in the planning stages,[29] but increased its financial support to the Pakistan-based Islamic parties through the military state of General Zia-ul-Haq, president of Pakistan.

When Premier Amin seized state and political power in September 1979 one of his main concerns was the consolidation of his power and the maintenance of stability. To achieve this he tried to normalize Afghanistan's relations with the United States and its bloc with a hope that the U.S. would cease its support to the Pakistan-based Islamic parties. According to a top secret memo from the U.S. embassy in Kabul to the Department of State, President Amin was sending friendly signals to the United States regarding this matter. The memo reads:

During the last seven days, we have been receiving clear signals that the DRA seeks better relations with us. I think it is important that these be appreciated. But I also believe it is too early to tell whether these signs will be substantiated in areas important to us. As we pointed out before to the Department, the DRA . . . [has] been conducting its policy towards us on two planes: on one level, they repeatedly inform us that the DRA wants better relations and that they consider the present situation "unnatural." Further, on this plane, they do such things as sending an unusually large number of ministers [3] to our July 4 reception, and most recently president and prime minister Hafizullah Amin received me warmly at the presidential palace. On the other hand, on another level, in areas more important to us, such as investigating Ambassador Dubs's death, and carrying out our Peace Corps, USAID and USICA programs, we have encountered many roadblocks. Additionally the government has over the last two months sought a reduction in the size of the U.S. embassy. In my view how we finally come out on this last issue will be the real test of their true intentions toward us.[30]

The United States did not trust President Amin and did not provide any political and economic support to his government on the grounds that President Amin had become thoroughly discredited and unpopular in Afghanistan and people hated him as a ruthless dictator. The United States continued providing financial support to the Pakistan-based Islamic parties in the hope that these parties would be able to serve U.S. interests in Afghanistan when they overthrow President Amin. Some of the Pakistan-based Islamic parties from the beginning of the popular uprising against the regime carried out a repressive policy against nationalist, revolutionary; and patriotic individuals throughout the country under the pretext of fighting "communism." Such a policy pursued by the Islamic parties, along with pervasive corruption within their rank and file, have isolated them from the people. The failure of Islamic parties to lead the popular uprising in the country resulted in the emergence of various revolutionary and nationalist forces that began to assert themselves as a social force capable of providing leadership to the movement in the country.

The U.S. embassy in Kabul wrote to the Department of State regarding this development and the consequence of U.S. support to the opposition forces in Afghanistan stating that

the victory of the opposition and the collapse of a pro-Soviet leftist radical regime would certainly serve the U.S. interest and it would show the Third World that the perspective of our rival Marxist-Leninists on the "inevitability" of world history is not necessarily true. A truly international non-aligned movement would be welcomed by us. The U.S. participation in economic construction would become possible in the case of the collapse of the DRA. However, there is no clear evidence on the programs of the opposition but inside the country a group of opposition parties Jabha-e-Milli-e-Enkilab Islami-e-Afghanistan (National Front for Islamic Revolution in Afghanistan) ostensibly supports the creation of a traditional Grand National Assembly to determine the future of Afghanistan. The U.S. would provide democratic support to such an organization if it truly comes into existence.[31]

This development in the movement in Afghanistan and the failure of the Islamic parties (who claim themselves *Amir* [leader] of the popular uprising prior to and after the Soviet invasion in December 1979) to unite, led the U.S. government to begin supporting veteran bureaucrats such as former King Zahir, former premier Mohammad Yusuf, etc., along with feudal landowners and top businessmen and other pro-Western technocrats in the hope that these forces would be able to provide a leadership to the uprising in Afghanistan.[32] The United States believed that the policies of the Pakistan-based Islamic parties do not serve the best interests of the United States in the region. A secret memo by the U.S. embassy in Kabul to the Department of State reads:

[T]he available manifesto issued by some opposition groups call for a social and economic system based on the "fundamentalist" tenets of Islam, and therefore, an opposition-led regime would probably not have social and economic reforms (so necessary for this backward country high on its priority list). Thousands of personal vendettas would probably be carried out against surviving Khalqi officials, thereby probably tarnishing a post- DRA regime's human rights record. No matter how justified retribution against some officials might appear to be.[33]

Since the pro-Western social forces did not succeed in asserting themselves in the resistance movement, the U.S. administration had no other
option but to work and support the Islamic parties.

Following the Soviet occupation of Afghanistan in December 1979
the U.S. administration increased its material and financial support to
the Pakistan-based Islamic parties. The U.S. administration considered
the Soviet invasion of Afghanistan as a potential threat to the U.S. long-
recognized spheres of influence, South Asia and the Persian Gulf regions. According to President Carter:

Our own nation's security was directly threatened. There is no doubt that the
Soviet's move into Afghanistan, if done without adverse consequences, would
have resulted in the temptation to move again until they reached warm water
ports or until they acquired control over a major portion of the world's oil
supplies.[34] . . . The Soviet Union has altered the strategic situation in that part
of the world in a very ominous fashion.[35] . . . It places the Soviets within
aircraft striking range of the vital oil resources of the Persian Gulf; it threatens
a strategically located country, Pakistan; [and] it poses the prospect of increased
Soviet pressure on Iran and on other nations of the Middle East.[36]

Former U.S. Secretary of State Henry Kissinger declared that the
United States must not appear weak or ineffectual against this threat to
their national interests. The Soviet Union must pay a price for its occupation of Afghanistan, and this price should be tied to such things as
the purchase of wheat and modern technology from the United States.
He said all U.S. commercial dealings with the Soviet Union should be
tied to its political and military conduct.[37] The Carter administration
subsequently boycotted the 1980 Olympics and imposed a grain embargo
against the Soviet Union.

Successive U.S. administrations also tried to use the Soviet invasion
of Afghanistan to mobilize world Muslim opinion against the Soviet
Union.[38] During a visit to Pakistan, George Shultz tried to advance the
U.S. position as the "natural ally" of national liberation movements
in countries dominated by the Soviet Union (similar to the Soviet policy
toward U.S. dominated countries). Shultz addressed a gathering of
refugees at a camp in Peshawar, near the Pakistani border with Afghanistan, saying:

This is a gathering in the name of freedom, a gathering in the name of self-
determination, a gathering in the name of getting the Soviet forces out of

Afghanistan, a gathering in the name of a sovereign Afghanistan controlled by its own people. Fellow fighters for freedom, we are with you.[39]

U.S. administration goals in supporting the resistance movement in Afghanistan were (a) making Afghanistan a "Soviet Vietnam"; (b) equating Communism with occupation, terror, and repression; and (c) mobilizing international opinion against Soviet expansionism.[40] To this end the U.S. government continually provided financial and military aid to the Pakistan-based Islamic parties. Such assistance, according to Charles Wilson, Democratic Representative of Texas meant that

there aren't going to be any more helicopters going back to Kabul with holes in them. They are going down. There were 58,000 dead in Vietnam and we owe the Russians one and you can quote me on that. I have had a slight obsession with it, because of Vietnam. I thought the Soviets ought to get a dose of it. I have been of the opinion that this money was better spent to hurt our adversaries than other money in the Defense Department.[41]

The U.S. government provided more than $625 million in aid (which is considered to be the largest CIA covert operation since the Vietnam War) to the Pakistan-based Islamic parties since December 1979.[42] In addition to the CIA's covert aid, the U.S. government provided a total of $430 million worth of commodities to refugees in Pakistan through international agencies[43] and continued providing military and financial support to the resistance forces in Afghanistan.

NOTES

1. *The Holy Quran*, Arabic Text, English Translation and Commentary by Maulana Muhammad Ali (Lahore: 1973), Section 3, Surah Zukhruf, Verse 32, p. 932.

2. Ibid., Surah Al-Nisa, Verse 71, p. 530.

3. M. Zaman Muzammil, *Reasons for the Russian Occupation and Dimensions of the Resistance in Afghanistan* (Peshawar: Hizbi Islami Afghanistan, 1979), p. 16.

4. Louis Dupree, "Population Dynamics in Afghanistan," *AUFS Reports*, 14 (1970):3.

5. Akhgar (Sazmani Mubariza Bara-e-Azadi Tabaqa-e-Kargar or Organization for Liberation of Working Class), *Afghanistan* (Tehran: 1980), p. 28.

6. *Jaraqa* (Urgani Tiyuriki Eitihadi Marksist-Lininista-e-Afghanistan or

Theoretical Organ of the Union of Marxist-Leninists of Afghanistan), 2 (September 1985):2.

7. Ibid., p. 6.

8. "U.S. Aid to Afghan Rebels is Largest Covert Operation Since Era of Vietnam War," *Washington Post*, 20 January 1985, pp. 15–17.

9. Mahfooz Ahmad, "Resistance Movement in Afghanistan: 1979–81," *Pakistan Horizon Quarterly* 36 (Third Quarter 1983):92; Bruce Amstutz, *Afghanistan: The First Five Years of Soviet Occupation* (Washington, DC: National Defense University, 1986), pp. 97–98.

10. Foreign Broadcast Information Service (FBIS), *Middle East and North Africa Daily Report* 6 March 1980, p. 2.

11. "Aims and Goals of Jamiati Islami-e-Afghanistan," *Mirror of Jihad* 1 (January-February 1982):10–11.

12. Eden Naby, "The Changing Role of Islam as a Unifying Force in Afghanistan," in *The State, Religion, and Ethnic Politics: Afghanistan, Iran, Pakistan* (Syracuse: Syracuse University Press, 1986), pp. 136–37.

13. Account by French Reporter Jean-Jose Puig in *Afghan Information Center Monthly Bulletin* (Peshawar: Pakistan) 32–33 (November-December 1983):27–28.

14. *Paris Le Monde*, 28–30 December 1983, in *JPRS Near East/South Asia Report*, 7 February 1984, p. 78.

15. *Jaraqa*, op. cit., no. 2, pp. 7–8.

16. General Union of Democratic Students and Patriotic Afghans (GUDSPA), *Independent Afghanistan* (San Francisco) 16 (November-December 1982):9.

17. Ibid., 3 (June 1981).

18. *Jaraqa*, op. cit., no. 5 (December 1985).

19. GUDSPA, *Independent Afghanistan*, op. cit., 3 (June 1981):2.

20. Ibid.

21. *The Tribune* (Oakland) 18 June 1980.

22. *Jaraqa*, op. cit., p. 9.

23. Akhgar, *Dar Sangari Mubariza wa Barnama-e-Ma Barai-e-Enkilabi Milli-Demokratik* [In the battlefield and our policy for national-democratic revolution] (Kabul: 1361 [1983]).

24. Afghanistan, Ministry of Planning, *Democratic Republic of Afghanistan Annual 1979* (Kabul: Government Printing House, 1979), p. 1,437.

25. Louis Dupree, *Afghanistan* (Princeton: Princeton University Press, 1973), p. 612.

26. *The Documents from the U.S. Espionage Den*, Section (1) Afghanistan (Tehran: Entisharat-e-Payami Azadi n.d.), p. 74.

27. "Afghanistan: 5 Years Later," *Revolutionary Workers*, 8 February 1985, pp. 6–8.

28. K. P. Misra, *Afghanistan in Crisis* (New Delhi: Vikas Publishing House, 1981), p. 54.

29. Ibid., p. 54.

30. *The Documents from the US Espionage Den*, op. cit., p. 100.

31. Ibid., p. 38. (Translated from Persian version of the document.)

32. GUDSPA, *Independent Afghanistan*, op. cit., vol. 3, (June 1981): p. 4.

33. *The Documents from the US Espionage Den*, op. cit., p. 31.

34. *Presidential Documents* 16 (14 January 1980):41.

35. *Presidential Documents* 16 (28 January 1980):165.

36. Ibid., p. 185.

37. *New York Times*, 4 January 1980.

38. B. K. Shrirastava, "The United States and Recent Developments in Afghanistan," in *Afghanistan in Crisis* (New Delhi: Vikas Publishing House, 1981), p. 56.

39. *Peoples Canada Daily News*, 7 July 1983, p. 4.

40. "Afghanistan 5 Years Later," *Revolutionary Workers*, op. cit.

41. *The Washington Post National Weekly Edition*, 28 January 1985, p. 14.

42. *The Guardian*, 17 February 1985.

43. U.S. Department of State, "Afghanistan: Six Years of Soviet Occupation," *Special Report*, no. 135, December 1985, p. 15.

5   Problems and Outlook

PEOPLE IN EXILE

People in Afghanistan began fleeing their homeland soon after the establishment of the "democratic" state in the country in April 1978. Among
the first refugees were members of the upper class and officials of the
previous government and others associated with them. They went to
Pakistan and from there some went on to Western European countries
and North America. More and more refugees fled Afghanistan when
the "democratic" state began to arrest and prosecute thousands of
suspected supporters of the opposition forces.

The Soviet military involvement in Afghanistan in December 1979
and the continuation of the war sent more waves of refugees to seek
shelter outside the country, mainly in Pakistan, Iran, the Middle East,
and Western European countries. According to United Nations statistics
there are 4.8 million refugees in Pakistan, Iran, and elsewhere as well
as one million internal refugees who fled the countryside to Kabul and
other major cities for security reasons. Approximately one-third of Af-

Note: An earlier verison of this chapter was published in *Cultural Survival Quarterly*
12(4):20-23 (December 1988). Reprinted with permission of Cultural Survival.

ghanistan's prewar population of 15 million has been uprooted and scattered; they represent one-half of the world's estimated refugee population.[1]

The state in Afghanistan before and after the Soviet military involvement in the country consistently denied the presence of refugees in the neighboring countries. Regarding the influx of refugees to Pakistan, President Babrak Karmal told a BBC correspondent during an interview that:

First, an important point: who has taken a census of these two or two and a half million people? These figures are entirely incorrect. But I would like to point out to you that throughout history two and a half and even three million Afghan nomads have been travelling to and from Afghanistan, previously to India, and presently to Pakistan. Likewise, there are Pushtun families having one brother living on this side and another brother on the other side, and they are travelling freely between the two countries.[2]

According to available statistics there are 2.7 million registered refugees in Pakistan living in 380 camps while several hundred thousand more are unregistered and live on their own resources. The overwhelming majority of refugees (75 percent) live in Pakistan's North West Frontier Province (NWFP), 20 percent in Baluchistan, and 4 percent in Punjab province.[3] Most of these refugees are Pushtu-speaking people from several southeastern provinces of the country. The majority of Pakistan-based refugees are followers of the Sunni sect of Islam.

According to the United Nations High Commissioner for Refugees (UNHCR), the latest official number of refugees from Afghanistan in the Islamic Republic of Iran is estimated to be 2.05 million (700,000 in Khurasan; 250,000 in Sistan-Baluchistan; 50,000 in Kerman; approximately 200,000 in Tehran; and 250,000 in Mashhad and the rest in nine other provinces). The refugee population also includes an estimated 200,000 people who had settled permanently in Iran prior to the Soviet invasion of Afghanistan and some 400,000 who were working in Iran at the time as seasonal laborers, tradesmen, and nomads. Most refugees work in various projects in Iran. Less than 50,000 refugees were accommodated in camps and other quarantine and reception centers.[4] Most of the refugees who settled in Iran are Persian-speaking people, Shiite in their religious orientation, and look to the Ayatollah Khomeini as the religious head of the Shiite sect in the Muslim world.

The Soviet occupation of Afghanistan and the continuation of nine years of war displaced almost all nationalities of the country. A major national group among Afghanistan refugees is the Pushtuns. Shortly after the Soviet invasion a great number of Pushtuns left their homes because their houses had been bombed and their properties destroyed. They crossed the Durand Line and settled in several areas in the North West Frontier Province (NWFP) of Pakistan, where they have relatives and distant kinfolk. They all share the same language, Pushtu. The government of Pakistan provided lodging and a limited amount of assistance to the refugees. As the number of refugees increased in subsequent years, the government of Pakistan appealed for international assistance and relocated refugees away from the border areas in Kurram and North Waziristan in the NWFP.

Refugees of other national groups such as the Hazara and Baluch are mainly concentrated in Quetta, capital of Baluchistan, Province of Pakistan. A great number of the Hazara ethnic group emigrated to Pakistan at the beginning of the twentieth century when the Hazara armed struggle for autonomy was crushed by the government; after their defeat many Hazaras were enslaved and their land awarded to Pushtun nomads.[5] Following the Soviet invasion, another wave of Hazara refugees poured into Quetta, Baluchistan, where they have distant relatives and kin. All speak Hazaragi, a dialect of the Persian language. Many other Hazara, who had no relatives in Pakistan, went to Iran because of their Shiite religious orientation.

A great number of Baluch people also left the country and settled in Quetta following the Soviet invasion where, like the Hazara, they have relatives and kinfolk. They are mainly Sunni in religous belief. A great number of those refugees who do not have relatives and are poor live in camps. Most refugees get a limited amount of food and their rations consist of flour, tea, and sugar. This situation compels children and the elderly to work in coal mines and construction projects in Baluchistan far below the wage level of a local Pakistani worker.[6]

The other major refugee groups are Uzbek, Tadjik, and Turkmen from the northern parts of the country. Unlike Pushtuns and Hazaras, these groups have no ethnic kinfolk in Pakistan. They speak their own languages (except the Tadjiks, who speak Persian). Almost 18,000 Uzbek and Tadjik refugees live in 320 villages established for them in Karachi, the capital of Sind Province of Pakistan. Getting employment in Karachi is difficult for the refugees because they cannot speak the languages of Urdu or Sindhi.[7]

Another group of refugees is the Kirghiz people from the Pamir district, Badakhshan province. They are Tadjiks and Ismaili in their religious orientations. They went to Gilgit, Pakistan, because a great number of Pakistanis in Gilgit belong to the same religious sect. Since these refugees are not settled in established refugee camps in the NWFP, Quetta or Karachi, they are not entitled to food stamps. They are poor and cannot afford to get medical treatment. They cope with various diseases such as malaria, hepatitis, and intestinal malfunctions. The government of Turkey granted refugee status to approximately 4,000 to 5,000 Kirghiz and other Turkic-speaking people in August 1982.[8] Refugees who settled in Pakistan can be classified into the following economic categories: landowners and businessmen, the intelligentsia, and peasants and laborers.

Landowners and Businessmen

This group of refugees constitutes a small section of the refugee population in Pakistan. They fled Afghanistan after the establishment of the "democratic" state in April 1978, bringing their cattle, personal belongings, vehicles, and money. According to the UNHCR's report, "a large number of the colored buses, painted trucks and auto-rickshaws that whiz in and out of traffic and along the national motorways are registered with this group of refugees."[9] The well-to-do refugees in Pakistan rented or bought fine suburban houses not only in Peshawar but also in Islamabad, Karachi, and other Pakistani cities. With the consolidation of an Islamic state in Iran and Islamicization of the state apparatuses in Pakistan this group of refugees saw no other option but to support the policies of the Islamic parties. When the government in Afghanistan closed the country's border with Pakistan a small number of drug-dealers and smugglers who used to operate (trade) between the two countries could no longer continue their business and protect their interests so they also settled in Pakistan and supported the Pakistan-based Islamic parties.

Intelligentsia

A large number of refugees in Pakistan are intellectuals (students, teachers, government officials, medical doctors, etc.) who left the country before and after the Soviet invasion. Most of these refugees espoused

Table 5.1
Estimated Number of Refugees, 1985

Country	Number
Pakistan	2,700,000
Iran	2,050,000
India	40,000
Western Europe	15,000
United States	7,106
Grand Total	4,812,106

Sources: United Nations, UNHCR, *Refugees*, December 1985; February 1986; May 1987.

Afghan nationalism and various trends of leftist radicalism and believed in a secular state in the aftermath of Soviet withdrawal from Afghanistan. The Pakistan-based Islamic parties in collaboration with the government of Pakistan limited the activities of these intellectuals among the refugees. Disgruntled with the situation in Pakistan, some of these refugees emigrated to India and to several West European countries. The United States also granted political asylum to high-ranking officials, pro-Western bureaucrats, and intellectuals of the previous government of Afghanistan. It also gave refugee status to individuals who either previously had studied in the United States, worked in U.S. agencies, or have immediate relatives (parents or siblings) residing in the United States. According to available statistics there are 7,106 Afghan refugees in the United States.[10]

Peasants and Laborers

The overwhelming majority of refugees are peasants and laborers who lost their houses and properties during the war and fled to Pakistan. A small number of skilled and semi-skilled refugees work as laborers in various development projects in Pakistan and compete with their Pakistani counterparts (see Table 5.1). As a result many laborers in Pakistan are beginning to resent the presence of refugees in their country. They increasingly blame refugees for higher rents, lower wages, and increased crime. According to an Afghan refugee, Pakistani resentment toward Afghan refugees is always present and "it corresponds to the bomb blasts. No matter where they happen, we suffer the affects. I went to Lahore shortly after the December riots in Karachi and was refused entry into several hotels. They told me it was because I am Afghan."[11]

The majority of the refugee population (75 percent) are women and children under age 15 and old men. In order to register for international aid all refugees must submit identification cards (ID) identifying themselves as members of either Islamic party. Otherwise they are not entitled to receive any kind of relief aid. Officials in charge of ration distribution among refugees get rich by appropriating the bulk of the refugee aid to themselves while the refugees barely survive in camps. Corruption is so pervasive that "in Baluchistan, a high official in charge of transport of refugee goods was court-martialed. Others at the highest level of responsibility have resigned rather than be brought up on charges. Despite the fact that these efforts have been widely publicized, outsiders persist in referring to the provincial administrative complexes as houses of 'thieves'."[12]

There are no educational opportunities for refugee children in Pakistan. Education for girls was considered anathema to the religious clerics and conservative tribal heads of the refugees in Pakistan. The precoup Afghan women who graduated from various educational institutions and occupied important positions in Afghanistan's administration now face the ire of ultraconservative religious and tribal leaders who seek to curtail the activities of women outside the home.

The majority of the combatants who battle the Soviet forces and the state in Afghanistan come from among this group of refugees. Although they are Muslim they don't articulate the Islamic aspect of the war but rather stress Afghan nationalism. However, leaders of the Islamic parties (in charge of arms and munitions in Pakistan) who have established themselves as representatives of the refugee population with the aid of Western countries try to identify the war in Afghanistan as a religious war—a war between "communism" and Islam.

SUPERPOWERS AND THE FUTURE OF AFGHANISTAN

The pattern of development and modernization in Afghanistan, unlike that in developing civil societies, did not generate from the bottom but was implemented from above by bureaucratic elites who tried to transform the country's precapitalist social formation overnight without creating a solid base to support it. The ruling class did not mobilize civilians to take an active part in carrying out the reforms. Lacking popular support and the active consent of civil society, the ruling class lost its consensus, that is, it was no longer the "leading" but only "dominant" influence, exercising coercive force alone. As a result the stage of development and the building of a modern society from above by the ruling class generated opposition among various social forces in the country. Lacking social support the ruling class was reduced to mere bureaucratic functionaries with no creative ideology binding them together in a legitimate social mandate. The struggle among various social forces to change and build a "democratic" society was threatening the ruling class in Afghanistan. In order to neutralize this growing counter-hegemonic force, the ruling class launched various development projects and turned to the superpowers—the United States and the Soviet Union—for technical and financial assistance.

The development strategy adopted improved living conditions for only a small section of the population in Afghanistan. As a result, dissatisfaction grew among various class factions within the state apparatus. This internal struggle within the state apparatus for power was further aggravated by U.S. and Soviet attempts to draw the country to their respective spheres of influence. The monarchy was overthrown in a coup in 1973 and Afghanistan was declared a republic. The ruling class, which held power, resorted to Islam to legitimize the new bureaucracy. It also promoted nationalism to deflect the influence of radical ideologies of the left and imprisoned key opposition leaders. In spite of all these measures the struggle of the opposition forces and other oppressed strata continued mounting during the five years of the republican regime. It was during this period that the republican regime was overthrown in a military coup in April 1978 and Afghanistan was declared a "democratic" republic.

The development strategies pursued by the "democratic" state antagonized conservative religious leaders, liberals, and nationalist forces in the country. Opposition to the regime began growing day by day. It grew stronger as the U.S. provided assistance to leaders of the Pakistan-based Islamic parties. The state in Kabul was not in a position to maintain political stability and was on the verge of collapse; in December 1979 the Soviet Union decided to send its troops not only to install a new leader, Babrak Karmal, but also to keep the country under its colonial domination.

The struggle among various class factions within the state apparatus and their alliance with the superpowers for military and financial assistance contributed to the continuation of the war in that country. In nine years of war neither did the Soviet Union succeed in consolidating the social base of the regime in Kabul, nor did the United States achieve a position sufficient to unify the Pakistan-based Islamic parties, to promote national strategies acceptable to various social forces in Afghanistan. During its nine-year occupation the Soviet Union failed to establish its influence in Afghanistan. They suffered 15,000 dead and 38,000 injured. Facing a stalemate and aware of a growing opposition both at home and abroad, the Soviet Union began to search for a means of a graceful exit from Afghanistan.

As a result of several years of mediation by the United Nations and high-level diplomatic dialogues between Soviet and U.S. officials an accord was reached encourging the governments of Afghanistan and Pakistan to sign an agreement of noninterference in each other's internal affairs. The agreement was signed by officials of Afghanistan and Pakistan and was endorsed by the two superpowers in Geneva on 14 May 1988. This gave the Soviets the opportunity to begin withdrawing its troops from Afghanistan within a nine-month period starting 15 May 1988.

Before the Soviet withdrawal is completed, the state in Kabul is trying everything possible to broaden its social base of support throughout the country. For this reason the state, through financial incentives or by involving influential tribal leaders in the decision-making body of the state apparatus, attempts to secure the participation of the people. In addition to this, the leadership in Kabul also has declared its readiness to share power with the leaders of the Pakistan-based Islamic parties if they return to Afghanistan. However, these resistance leaders verbally rejected the Geneva Accord and the call of the government in Kabul for a coalition government of national reconciliation and vowed to fight until they overthrow the state in Kabul and establish an Islamic state in its place.

The refugee population who endured nine years of hardship in squalid refugee camps in Pakistan is still not happy with the policies and practices of the Islamic parties regarding the treatment of refugees in Pakistan. While these refugees may return to Afghanistan before the Soviet withdrawal is completed, "the Mujahidin coalition strongly opposes any refugee return until the Soviet withdrawal is completed. They see it will be unsafe for civilians to go home until then, more likely, they fear that their own influence will decline once refugees start to return to their traditional villages and district environments."[13]

The state in Kabul called upon refugees and other exiled Afghan nationals to return home and declared that returnees will be provided every possible assistance for their resettlement. Both the government in Afghanistan and the Pakistan-based Islamic parties see the refugees as a potentially strong political weapon. Each tries to broaden its social and political influence among them by permitting the flow of international aid and its distribution among the refugees when the Soviets begin to leave and refugees begin returning to Afghanistan.

Although the United States and the Soviet Union endorsed the Geneva Accord, they have not yet agreed to recognize an Afghanistan independent of superpower spheres of influence. Thus they continue their struggle for hegemony in Afghanistan through their cliental social forces—the pro-Soviet People's Democratic Party of Afghanistan (PDPA) and the pro-U.S. Pakistan-based Islamic parties. The struggle between these two social forces for state and political power in Afghanistan will continue until one of the contending parties emerges victorious or the existing independent progressive organizations in the country succeed in leading the struggle of the people for an independent Afghanistan free from the influence of both superpowers.

NOTES

1. United Nations, United Nations High Commissioner For Refugees (UNHCR), *Refugees*, February 1986, p. 9.

2. Afghanistan, Ministry of Foreign Affairs, *White Book: Foreign Policy Documents of the Democratic Republic of Afghanistan* (Kabul: Government Printing House, 1985), p. 11.

3. United Nations, UNHCR, *Refugees*, op. cit., p. 9.

4. Ibid., February 1987, pp. 10–11.

5. Hasan Kakar, *Government and Society in Afghanistan: Reign of Abd al Rahman*. (Austin: Austin University Press, 1979).

6. United Nations, UNHCR, *Refugees*, May 1986, p. 18.

7. Ibid., February 1987, p. 27.

8. Ibid., February 1982.

9. Ibid., May 1987, p. 20.

10. *Refugee Reports* 6 (December 1985):9.

11. United Nations, UNHCR, *Refugees*, op. cit., May 1987, p. 20.

12. Nancy Dupree, ''The Demography of Afghan Refugees in Pakistan,'' in *Soviet-American Relations with Pakistan, Iran and Afghanistan* (Hampshire and London: The Macmillan Press, 1987), p. 374.

13. *Christian Science Monitor*, 24 May 1988, p. 16.

Postscript

Afghanistan was regarded as one of the underdeveloped societies in Asia prior to the Soviet intervention in December 1979. The Soviet occupation and the nine-year war has paralyzed the country's economy, stalled its social development, and decimated its population. Of 22,000 towns, approximately 12,000 have been destroyed; 60 percent of all health centers have been demolished by the war. It is estimated that 1.24 million people have been killed, two million displaced from villages and towns to major cities for security reasons and 4.8 million forced to seek refuge in the neighboring countries of Iran and Pakistan.

In the struggle to establish their hegemony in Afghanistan, the United States and the Soviet Union not only provided military support to their clients—the Pakistan-based Islamic Parties and the People's Democratic Party of Afghanistan (PDPA) respectively—they also used the country as a testing ground for their new military equipment and modern weaponry. The Soviet Union tested its military equipment: assault rifles, automatic grenade launchers, multiple-rocket launchers, combat vehicles, etc., and the United States tested the Stinger anti-aircraft missiles on Soviet combat aircraft and other high-tech weapons.

During nine years of war in Afghanistan the Soviet Union failed to sustain its colonial domination of Afghanistan and was compelled to withdraw its troops from the country in February 1989. Following the Soviet troop withdrawal, the PDPA and the Islamic parties (collectively known as *Mujahidin*), vowed to fight for control of the country's future. Both the PDPA and the *Mujahidin* lack popular support, although each claims to enjoy an overwhelming support of the majority of the people in the country.

To consolidate its position the leadership in Kabul adopted two distinct policies: (a) a military strategy, in which the government withdrew its armed forces from peripheral locations throughout the country and concentrated them in several major cities in order to maintain these cities under its control and to avoid military casualties in regions which had no strategic significance; and (b) a political strategy, where the government declared the peripheral areas autonomous and called upon tribal leaders to undertake the administration of these regions.

The prime objective of the leadership in Kabul in withdrawing its forces from non-strategic areas, granting autonomy to these regions (areas which either had been abandoned by the regime or had been occupied by the people in the war) and permitting opponents and refugees to return and assume the administration of the regions is to exploit contradictions among various contending Islamic parties over the administration of the territories. The regime in Kabul believes that its position in the country would be enhanced by fueling contradiction and inciting internal struggle among the Islamic parties.

The government tries to intensify hostilities among the Islamic parties and the tribal leaders and further alienate them from people who oppose the Islamic parties and their strategies of political and social development. Opposition forces in Kabul, comprised of a wide spectrum of middle and lower-class people, not only oppose the government in Kabul but also despise the strategies of the Islamic parties, including their missile attacks on civilian areas, and their economic blockades of the city. During the severe cold winter of February–March 1989, the Islamic parties imposed a blockade of Kabul. Temperatures plummeted below zero and food and fuel were dangerously scarce. While the blockade took a heavy toll among the city's inhabitants, it had little impact on the state's apparatus and its leaders.

Refugees in the neighboring countries of Iran and Pakistan are dissatisfied with the policies of the Islamic parties, which to them seem to be more inclined toward a struggle for political power rather than a fight to improve the lot of the people of Afghanistan. The peasantry also suffer from the erratic and arbitrary taxation systems imposed on it by various Islamic parties and tribal leaders as well as from the physical destruction of their agricultural land by military attack.

Since tribalism and regionalism supersede the national character of the war, the regime in Kabul is attempting to exploit tribal and ethnic differences to its advantage. The regime maintains that granting autonomy to various regions would further promote tribalism and regionalism and would erode the influence of the Islamic parties. With the intent of more firmly securing its position, the leadership in Kabul is trying to further discredit its adversaries—the *Mujahidin*—by exaggerating their relations with the West and portraying them as Western agents.

The struggle between the regime in Kabul and the Islamic parties over the future of Afghanistan in the post-Soviet withdrawal period continues; neither side has paid much attention to the daunting matter of the reconstruction of Afghanistan's economy, political institutions and social development. Even if a resolution of this war were to be achieved, there will be no immediate end to feuds, factionalism and armed struggle in the country. The large numbers of internal and external refugees will still have to deal with the long and arduous task of resettling and rebuilding their lives.

Appendix: Text of Afghanistan-Pakistan Accord

U.S., USSR ALSO PLEDGE NON-INTERVENTION

Bilateral Agreement Between the Republic of Afghanistan and the Islamic Republic of Pakistan on the Principles of Mutual Relations, in particular on Non-Interference and Non-Intervention

The Republic of Afghanistan and the Islamic Republic of Pakistan, hereinafter referred to as the High Contracting Parties;

Desiring to normalize relations and promote good-neighborliness and co-operation as well as to strengthen international peace and security in the region;

Considering that full observance of the principle of non-interference and non-intervention in the internal and external affairs of States is of the greatest importance for the maintenance of international peace and security and for the fulfillment of the purposes and principles of the Charter of the United Nations;

Re-affirming the inalienable right of States freely to determine their own political, economic, cultural and social systems in accordance with the will of their peoples, without outside intervention, interference, subversion, coercion or threat in any form whatsoever;

Mindful of the provisions of the Charter of the United Nations as well as the resolutions adopted by the United Nations on the principle of non-interference and non-intervention, in particular the Declaration on Principles of International

Law concerning Friendly Relations and Cooperation among States in accordance with the Charter of the United Nations, of 24 October 1970, as well as the Declaration on the Inadmissibility of Intervention and Interference in the Internal Affairs of States, of 9 December 1981; Have agreed as follows:

Article I

Relations between the High Contracting parties shall be conducted in strict compliance with the principle of non-interference and non-intervention by States in the affairs of other States.

Article II

For the purpose of implementing the principle of non-interference and non-intervention each High Contracting Party undertakes to comply with the following obligations:

(1) to respect the sovereignty, political independence, territorial integrity, national unity, security and non-alignment of the other High Contracting Party, as well as the national identity and cultural heritage of its people;

(2) to respect the sovereign and inalienable right of the other High Contracting Party freely to determine its own political, economic, cultural and social systems, to develop its international relations and to exercise permanent sovereignty over its natural resources, in accordance with the will of its people, and without outside intervention, interference, subversion, coercion or threat in any form whatsoever;

(3) to refrain from the threat or use of force in any form whatsoever so as not to violate the boundaries of each other, to disrupt the political, social or economic order of the other High Contracting Party, to overthrow or change the political system of the other High Contracting Party or its Government, or to cause tension between the High Contracting Parties;

(4) to ensure that its territory is not used in any manner which would violate the sovereignty, political independence, territorial integrity and national unity or disrupt the political, economic and social stability of the other High Contracting Party;

(5) to refrain from armed intervention, subversion, military occupation or any other form of intervention and interference, overt or covert, directed at the other High Contracting Party, or any act of military, political or economic interference in the internal affairs of the other High Contracting Party, including acts of reprisal involving the use of force;

(6) to refrain from any action or attempt in whatever form or under whatever pretext to destabilize or to undermine the stability of the other High Contracting Party or any of its institutions;

(7) to refrain from the promotion, encouragement or support, direct or indirect, of rebellious or secessionist activities against the other High Contracting

Party, under any pretext whatsoever, or from any other action which seeks to disrupt the unity or to undermine or subvert the political order of the other High Contracting Party;

(8) to prevent within its territory the training, equipping, financing and recruitment of mercenaries from whatever origin for the purpose of hostile activities against the other High Contracting Party, or the sending of such mercenaries into the territory of the other High Contracting Party and accordingly to deny facilities, including financing for the training, equipping and transit of such mercenaries;

(9) to refrain from making any agreements or arrangements with other States designed to intervene or interfere in the internal and external affairs of the other High Contracting Party;

(10) to abstain from any defamatory campaign, vilification or hostile propaganda for the purpose of intervening or interfering in the internal affairs of the other High Contracting Party;

(11) to prevent any assistance to or use of or tolerance of terrorist groups, saboteurs or subversive agents against the other High Contracting Party;

(12) to prevent within its territory the presence, harboring, in camps and bases or otherwise, organizing, financing, equipping and arming of individuals and political, ethnic and any other groups for the purpose of creating subversion, disorder or unrest in the territory of the other High Contracting Party and accordingly also to prevent the use of mass media and the transportation of arms, ammunition and equipment by such individuals and groups;

(13) not to resort to or to allow any other action that could be considered as interference or intervention.

Article III

The present Agreement shall enter into force on 15 May 1988.

Article IV

Any steps that may be required in order to enable the High Contracting Parties to comply with the provisions of Article II of this Agreement shall be completed by the date on which this Agreement enters into force.

Article V

This Agreement is drawn up in the English, Pushtu and Urdu languages, all texts being equally authentic. In case of any divergence of interpretation, the English text shall prevail.

Done in five original copies at Geneva this fourteenth of April 1988.

(Signed by Afghanistan and Pakistan)

DECLARATION ON INTERNATIONAL GUARANTEES

The Governments of the Union of Soviet Socialist Republics and of the United States of America,

Expressing support that the Republic of Afghanistan and the Islamic Republic of Pakistan have concluded a negotiated political settlement designed to normalize relations and promote good-neighborliness between the two countries as well as to strengthen international peace and security in the region;

Wishing in turn to contribute to the achievement of the objectives that the Republic of Afghanistan and the Islamic Republic of Pakistan have set themselves, and with a view to ensuring respect for their sovereignty, independence, territorial integrity and non-alignment;

Undertake to invariably refrain from any form of interference and intervention in the internal affairs of the Republic of Afghanistan and the Islamic Republic of Pakistan and to respect the commitments contained in the bilateral Agreement between the Republic of Afghanistan and the Islamic Republic of Pakistan on the Principles of Mutual Relations, in particular on Non-Interference and Non-Intervention;

Urge all States to act likewise.

The present Declaration shall enter into force on 15 May 1988. Done at Geneva, this fourteenth day of April 1988 in five original copies, each in the English and Russian language, both texts being equally authentic.

(Signed by the USSR and the USA)

Source: *Mainichi Daily News* (Japan), 15 April 1988, p. C 3.

Selected Bibliography

BOOKS

On Economics

Afghanistan. Ministry of Planning. *Survey of Progress 1962–1964*. Kabul: Government Printing House, 1964.

———. Ministry of Planning. *Survey of Progress 1967–1968*. Kabul: Government Printing House, 1968.

———. Ministry of Planning. *Survey of Progress 1969–1970*. Kabul: Government Printing House, 1970.

———. Ministry of Planning. *Statistical Pocketbook of Afghanistan 1350*. Kabul: Government Printing House, 1350 [1971].

———. Ministry of Planning. *Afghan Agriculture in Figures, Qaus 1357*. Kabul: Government Printing House, 1978.

———. Ministry of Planning. *Democratic Republic of Afghanistan Annual 7 Saur 1358*. Kabul: Government Printing House, 1979.

Amin, Hamidullah and Schilz, B. Gordon. *A Geography of Afghanistan*. Omaha: Center for Afghanistan Studies, 1976.

Anderson, Clay. *A Banking and Credit System for Economic Development of Afghanistan*. Washington, DC: Robert Nathan Associates, 1967.

Area Handbook for Afghanistan. Pamphlet 550–65. Washington, DC: The American University, 1969.

Byroade, H. A. *The Changing Position of Afghanistan in Asia*. Publication no. 7142. Washington: Department of State, 1961.

Central Intelligence Agency (CIA). *Handbook of Economic Statistics 1983*, September 1983.

Chernyakovskaya, Neonila. *Development of Industry and Position of the Working Class of Afghanistan*. Moscow: Nauka Publishing Co., 1965.

Ekker, Martin. *Economic Aspects of Development of Afghanistan*. New York: United Nations, 1952.

Franck, P. G. *Afghanistan Between East and West: The Economics of Competitive Coexistence*. Washington, DC: National Planning Association, 1960.

Fraser-Tytler, W. K. *Afghanistan: A Study of Political Development in Central and Southern Asia*. London: Oxford University Press, 1967.

Fry, Maxwell J. *Afghan Economy: Money, Finance, and the Critical Constraints to Economic Development*. Leiden: Brill, 1974.

Gregorian, Vartan. *The Emergence of Modern Afghanistan: Politics of Reform and Modernization*. Palo Alto: Stanford University, 1969.

Kakar, Hasan. *Government and Society in Afghanistan: Reign of Abd al Rahman*. Austin: Austin University Press, 1979.

Kamrany, Nake M. *Peaceful Competition in Afghanistan: American and Soviet Models for Economic Aid*. Washington, DC: Communications Service Corporation, 1969.

Nyberg, Howard. *An Analysis of Private Investment in Afghanistan*. Chicago: Miner and Associates, 1966.

The Quarterly Economic Review: Pakistan, Bangladesh and Afghanistan. London: The Economist Intelligence Unit. 1974; 1975; 1967; 1977; 1985.

Scherer, John. *USSR. Facts and Figures Annual 1981*. Gulf Breeze: Academic International Press, 1981.

Sikoyev, Ruslan. *Firm Friends for 60 Years: Sixty Years of Diplomatic Relations Between the USSR and Afghanistan*. Moscow: Novosti Press Agency, 1979.

Strauss, A. A. *Industrial Development in Afghanistan: A Forward Look*. Kabul: Robert and Nathan Associates, 1965.

Surkha (Sazmani Rahayi Bakhshi Khalqa-e-Afghanistan or Organization for Liberation of the People of Afghanistan). *Chegunagi-e-Paidayish wa Rushdi Bourgeoisie dar Afghanistan* [The process and development of bourgeoisie in Afghanistan]. Kabul: Ayendagan Press, 1980.

Trosper, Joseph F. *The States of Insurance in Afghanistan*. Bloomington: Indiana University, 1972.

United Nations, United Nations High Commission for Refugees (UNHCR). *Refugees*. May 1987; October 1981; December 1985; February 1986.

U.S. Department of Commerce. *Obtaining Financial Aid for a Development*

Plan: *The Export-Import Bank of Washington Loans to Afghanistan*. September 30, 1953.

U.S. Department of Commerce, Bureau of Foreign Commerce, Trade Mission Division. *Report to the U.S. Trade Mission to Afghanistan*. 20 August–10 September 1960.

U.S. Embassy. *Annual Economic Trends Reports*. Kabul: June 1970.

U.S., USAID-Afghanistan. *Status of All Projects Financed by Foreign Aid for Afghanistan's Development*. Kabul: USAID, 1970.

Watkins, Mary Bradly. *Afghanistan Land in Transition*. Princeton: Van Nostrand, 1963.

Whittlesey, Norman K. *The Marketing System of Afghanistan*. Kabul: USAID, 1967.

World Bank. *Afghanistan: The Journey to Economic Development*. The Main Report, vol. 1, Report No. 1777a-af (17 March 1978).

Zhowandai, Saleha. "An Economic Analysis and Measurement of Afghanistan's Protection Structure." Ph.D Diss., University of Hawaii-Manoa, 1977.

On Government and Politics

Afghanistan. The Kabul Times Publishing Agency. *The Kabul Times Annual 1967*. Kabul: Government Printing House, 1967.

————. The Kabul Times Publishing Agency. *Afghanistan Republic Annual 1975*. Kabul: Government Printing House, 1975.

————. The Kabul Times Publishing Agency. *Afghanistan Republic Annual 1976*. Kabul: Government Printing House, 1976.

————. Ministry of Education. *Constitution of Afghanistan 1964*. Kabul: Franklin Book Programs, 1964.

————. Ministry of Planning. *Majmuaei Aisayawi-e-Sali 1350* [Statistical dictionary of 1971]. Kabul: Matbaa-e-Dawlati, 1350 [1971].

Akhgar (Sazmani Mubariza Bara-e-Azadi Tabaqa-e-Kargar or Organization for Liberation of Working Class). *Afghanistan*. Tehran: 1980.

————. *Auza-e-Kununi Wa Maukiyati Ma* [The present condition and our position]. N.p. 1360 [1982].

————. *Dar Sangari Mubariza wa Barnama-e-Ma Bari-e-Enkilabi Milli-Demokratik* [In the battlefield and our policy for national-democratic revolution]. Kabul: 1361 [1983].

Ali, Banuazizi, and Myron Weiner, eds. *The State, Religion and Ethnic Politics: Afghanistan, Iran and Pakistan*. Syracuse: Syracuse University Press, 1986.

Ali, Mohammad. *Afghanistan: The National Awakening*. Lahore: Punjab Publication Press, 1958.

Amnesty International Report. London: Amnesty International Publications, 1980.

Amstutz, Bruce J. *Afghanistan: The First Five Years of Soviet Occupation*. Washington, DC: National Defense University, 1986.

Anwar, Raja. *The Tragedy of Afghanistan*. London and New York: Verso, 1988.

Arnold, Anthony. *Afghanistan: The Soviet Invasion in Perspective*. Stanford: Hoover Institution Press, 1981.

————. *Afghanistan's Two-Party Communism—Parcham and Khalq*. Stanford: Hoover Institution, 1983.

Azoy, Whitney G. *Buzkashi: Game and Power in Afghanistan*. Philadelphia: University of Pennsylvania Press, 1982.

Bhaneja, Balwart. *Afghanistan: Political Modernization of a Mountain Kingdom*. New Delhi: Spectra Publications, 1973.

Bhargave, G. S. *South Asian Security After Afghanistan*. Washington, DC: Lexington Books, 1983.

Bhasin, V. K. *Superpower Rivalry in the Indian Ocean*. New Delhi: S. Chand and Co. Ltd., 1981.

————. *Soviet Intervention in Afghanistan*. New Delhi: S. Chand and Co. Ltd., 1984.

Bradsher, Henry S. *Afghanistan and the Soviet Union*. Durham: Duke University Press, 1983, 1985.

Burrel, R. M., and Alvin J. Cottrell. *Iran, Afghanistan, and Pakistan: Tension and Dilemmas*. Beverly Hills: Sage Publications, 1974.

Chakravarty, Subhash. *From Khyber to Oxus: A Study in Imperial Expansion*. New Delhi: Orient Longmans, 1976.

Collins, Joseph J. *The Soviet Invasion of Afghanistan: A Study in the Use of Force in Soviet Foreign Policy*. Massachusetts: Lexington Books, 1986.

Documents From The U.S. Espionage Den, The. Section (1) Afghanistan. By Muslim Students Following the Line of the Imam. Tehran: Entisharat-e-Payami Azadi (with Persian Translation), n.d.

Eberhard, Welfram. *Afghanistan's Young Elite*. Hong Kong: Hong Kong University Press, 1967.

Elmi, S.M.Y., and S. B. Majrooh. *The Sovietization of Afghanistan*. Peshawar: Afghan Jihad Works, Translation Center, 1986.

General Union of Democratic Students and Patriotic Afghans (GUDSPA). *Pasikh ba Sazmani Fidayian-e-Mujahidini Karaj dar Iran* [A response to the organization of the Fidayian-e-Mujahid of Karaj in Iran], N.p., n.d.

Gharjistani, Mohammad Isa. *Shikasti Rus-ha dar Hazarajat* [The Russian defeat in Hazarajat]. Bonn: Eitihadiya-e-Muhassilan wa Afghanan dar Bon, 1981.

————. *Kalamunarha dar Afghanistan* [Human minarets in Afghanistan]. Quetta: Pakistan, n.d.

Ghosh, Ramesh Chandra. *Constitutional Documents of the Major Islamic States*. Lahore: Muhammad Ashraf, 1947.

Giradet, Edward. *Afghanistan: The Soviet War*. New York: St. Martin's Press, 1985.

Grassmuck, George, Ludwig Adamec, and Frances H. Irwin. *Afghanistan: Some New Approaches*. Ann Arbor: The University of Michigan, 1969.

Hammond, Thomas T. *Red Flag Over Afghanistan*. Boulder: Westview Press, 1984.

Harkishan, Surjeet S. *Development in Afghanistan*. New Delhi: Communist Party of India (ML), Progressive Printers, 1982.

Hyman, Anthony. *Afghanistan Under Soviet Domination 1964–83*. New York: St. Martin's Press, 1984.

Khrushchev, Nikita. *Khrushchev Remembers*. Boston: Little, Brown, 1970.

Larson, Thomas. *Soviet-American Rivalry*. New York: Norton, 1978.

Male, Beverley. *Revolutionary Afghanistan: A Reappraisal*. New York: St. Martin's Press, 1982.

Malik, Hafeez, ed. *Soviet-American Relations with Pakistan, Iran and Afghanistan*. Hampshire and London: The Macmillan Press Ltd., 1987.

Monks, Alfred L. *The Soviet Intervention in Afghanistan*. Washington, DC: American Enterprise Institute, 1981.

Mukherjee, Sadhan. *Afghanistan from Tragedy to Triumph*. New Delhi: Sterling Publishers Private Ltd., 1984.

Nazaar, Fazil. "Development, Modernization and Leadership Style in Afghanistan: A Human-Simulation in Politics." Ph.D diss., University of Hawaii-Manoa, 1972.

Newell, Richard S. *The Politics of Afghanistan*. Ithaca: Cornell University Press, 1972.

Newell, Richard, and Nancy P. Newell. *The Struggle for Afghanistan*. Ithaca and London: Cornell University Press, 1981.

Pazhwak, Ahmad. *Modern Afghanistan*. Kabul: Kabul University Press, 1965.

Poullada, Leon B. *Reform and Rebellion in Afghanistan 1919–1929*. Ithaca and London: Cornell University Press, 1973.

Rahel, Shafie. *Cultural Policy in Afghanistan*. Paris: The UNESCO Press, 1975.

Ratnam. *Afghanistan's Uncertain Future*. New Delhi: Tulsi Publishing House, 1981.

Rubinstein, Alvin Z. *Soviet Foreign Policy Since World War II: Imperial and Global*. Boston: Little, Brown & Co., 1984.

Sazmani-Nasr (Nasr Organization). *Naft wa Gaz dar Afghanistan wa Gharatgariha-e-Imperializmi Shorawi* [Oil and gas in Afghanistan and the exploitation of Russian imperialism]. Tehran: Entisharati Balkhi, 1359 [1981].

Sen-Gupta, Bhabani. *USSR in Asia: An Interperceptional Study of Soviet-Asian Relations With a Critique of Soviet Role in Afghanistan.* New Delhi: Vikas Publishing House, 1980.

―――. *The Afghan Syndrome: How to Live with Soviet Power.* New Delhi: Vikas Publishing House, 1982.

Silber, Irwin. *Afghanistan: The Battle Line is Drawn.* San Francisco: Line of March Publications, 1980.

Silvert, K. H. *Expectant Peoples: Nationalism and Development.* New York: Random House, 1963.

Steel, J. *World Powers: Soviet Foreign Policy Under Brezhnev and Andropov.* London: Michael Joseph, 1983.

Taraki, Noor M. "The Basic Lines of Revolutionary Duties of the Democratic Republic of Afghanistan." *Democratic Republic of Afghanistan Annual 7 Saur 1358* (Kabul: The Kabul Times Publishing Agency, 1979).

U. S. Congress. House. Committee on Foreign Affairs Hearing. *82nd Cong.*, 1st sess., 1951.

U. S. Department of State. *Foreign Relations of the United States 1949.* Vol. 6. Washington, DC: Government Printing House, 1977.

―――. *Foreign Relations of the United States 1951.* Vol. 5. Washington, DC: Government Printing House, 1977.

―――. *Foreign Relations of the United States 1952–54.* Vol. 11. Washington, DC: Government Printing House, 1977.

U.S.S.R. *The Truth About Afghanistan-Documents, Facts, Eyewitness Reports.* Moscow: Novosti Press Agency, 1980.

Valian, Abdul Azim. *Kuliyati az Auwzayi Siyasi wa Eiktisadi wa Eijtimaei Afghanistan* [A collection of notes on political, social and economic situation in Afghanistan]. Tehran: Zawar Publication, 1961.

Van Dyke, Jere. *In Afghanistan: An American Odyssey.* New York: Coward-McCann, 1983.

Vance, Cyrus. *Hard Choices: Critical Years in America's Foreign Policy.* New York: Simon and Schuster, 1983.

Wakman, Mohammad Amin. *Afghanistan Non-Alignment and the Superpowers.* New Delhi: Radiant Publishers, 1985.

―――. *Afghan Social Democratic Party.* New Delhi: Public House, 1985.

On History

Adamec, Ludwig W. *Afghanistan's Foreign Affairs to the Mid-Twentieth Century.* Tucson: University of Arizona Press, 1974.

―――. *Afghanistan 1900–1921: A Diplomatic History.* Berkeley: University of California Press, 1976.

Afghanistan. Royal Afghan Embassy in London. *Afghanistan News*, 6 June 1963.

————. Ministry of Planning. *Afghanistan, Ancient Land with Modern Ways*. Kabul: Government Printing House, 1966.

————. Ministry of Foreign Affairs. *White Book: Foreign Policy Documents of the Democratic Republic of Afghanistan*. Kabul: Government Printing House, 1985.

Ahang. M. *A Short History of Journalism in Afghanistan*. Kabul: Government Printing House, 1970.

Akhramovich, R. T. *Outline History of Afghanistan After Second World War*. Moscow: Nauka Publishing Co., 1966.

Ali, Mohammad. *The Mohammadzai Period*. Kabul: Kabul University Press, 1959.

————. *Progressive Afghanistan*. Lahore: Punjab Educational Press, 1970.

————. *A Short History of Afghanistan*. Kabul: Punjab Educational Press, 1970.

Amin, Tahir. *Afghanistan in Crisis*. Islamabad: Institute of Policy Studies, 1982.

Chiland, Gerard. *Report from Afghanistan*. New York: Penguin Books, 1982.

Dupree, Louis. *Afghanistan*. Princeton: Princeton University Press, 1973.

Dupree, Louis, and Albert Linette, eds. *Afghanistan in the 1970s*. New York, Washington and London: Praeger Publishers, 1974.

Fletcher, Arnold. *Afghanistan: Highway to Conquest*. Ithaca: Cornell University Press, 1965.

Gankovsky, V. Yu, M. R. Arunova, V. G. Korgun, V. M. Musson, G. A. Muradov, G. A. Polyakov, and V. A. Romodin. *A History of Afghanistan*. Translated by Vitaly Bashkakov. Moscow: Progress Publishers, 1985.

Ghaus, Abdul Samad. *The Fall of Afghanistan* (Virginia: Pergamon-Brassey's International Defense Publishers, 1988).

Ghubar, Mir Ghulam Mohammad. *Afghanistan dar Masir-e-Tarikh* [Afghanistan in the path of history]. Kabul: Government Printing House, 1967.

Griffiths, T. G. *Afghanistan*. New York-Washington: Praeger Publishers, 1967.

————. *Afghanistan*. Boulder: Westview Press, 1981.

Gupta, Anand. *Lenin and India*. New Delhi: New Literatures, 1980.

Harrison, Selig S. *In Afghanistan's Shadow*. New York: Carnegie Endowment for International Peace, 1981.

Holy Quran, Arabic Text, English Translation and Commentary by Maulana Muhammad Ali. Lahore, 1973.

Misra, K. P., ed. *Afghanistan in Crisis*. New Delhi: Vikas Publishing House, 1981.

Muzammil, Zaman M. *Reasons for the Russian Occupation and Dimensions of the Resistance in Afghanistan*. Peshawar: Hizbi Islami of Afghanistan, 1979.

Nayar, Kuldip. *Report on Afghanistan.* New Delhi: Vikas Publishing House, 1981.

Nollau, Gunther, and Hans Jurgen Whehe. *Russia: South Flank: Soviet Operation in Iran, Turkey and Afghanistan.* New York: Praeger Publishers, 1963.

U.S.S.R. *Afghanistan: Past and Present.* Moscow: USSR Academy of Sciences, Oriental Studies in the U.S.S.R., no. 3, 1981.

ARTICLES

On Economics

Anderson, Jon W. "There Are No More Khans Any More: Economic Development and Social Change in Tribal Afghanistan." *Middle East Journal* 32 (Spring 1978): 167–84.

Bechhoefer, William. "Architectural Education in Afghanistan." *Afghanistan Journal* (Jg. 4, Heft 4, 1977): 147–49.

Bradsher, Henry. "Stagnation and Change in Afghanistan." *Journal of South Asian and Middle Eastern Studies* 10 (Fall 1986): 3–35.

Brant, Marvin. "Recent Economic Development." In *Afghanistan in the 1970s* (New York: Praeger Publishers, 1974), pp. 91–112.

Charpentier, C. J. "One Year After the Saur Revolution." *Afghanistan Journal* (Jg. 67, Heft 4, 1979): 17–19.

Dupree, Louis. "American Private Enterprise in Afghanistan: The Investment Climate, Particularly as it Relates to One Company." *AUFS Reports* 4 (December 1960): 1–15.

———. "Afghanistan in the Twentieth Century." *Journal of the Royal Central Asian Society* 2 (January 1965): 21–29.

———. "The Emergence of Technocrats in Modern Afghanistan: Changing Patterns of Socio-political Stratification: 1880–1973." *AUFS Reports* 18 (August 1974): 1–15.

———. "A Note on Afghanistan: 1974." *AUFS Reports* 18 (September 1974): 1–17.

———. "Afghanistan 1977: Does Trade Plus Aid Guarantee Development?" *AUFS Reports* 21 (August 1977): 1–13.

Farid, F. R. "The Modernization of Afghanistan." *Afghanistan* 17 (July-August-September 1962): 7–22.

Forr, Grant M., and Azam Gul. "Afghanistan's Agricultural Production 1978–1982." *Journal of South Asian and Middle Eastern Studies* 8 (Fall 1984): 65–79.

Gibbs, David. "The Peasant as Counter-Revolutionary: The Rural Origins of the Afghan Insurgency." *Studies in Comparative International Development* 21 (Spring 1986): 36–59.

Guha, Almalendu. "Economic Development of Afghanistan 1929–1961." *International Studies* 6 (April 1965): 421–31.

———. "The Economy of Afghanistan During Amanullah's Reign." *International Studies* 9 (October 1967): 61–82.

Michel, A. A. "Foreign Trade and Foreign Policy in Afghanistan." *Middle Eastern Affairs* 12 (January 1961): 7–10.

Miranov, L., and G. Polyakov. "Afghanistan: Beginning of a New Life." *International Affairs* 3 (March 1979): 46–54.

Noorzoy, M. S. "Planning and Growth in Afghanistan." *World Development* 4 (September 1976): 671–75.

———. "An Analysis of the Afghan Foreign and Domestic Investment Law of 1974." *Afghanistan Journal* (Jg. 4, Heft 1, 1979): 29–30.

———. "Soviet Economic Interests in Afghanistan." *Problems of Communism* 36 (May-June 1981): 43–54.

———. "Long-Term Economic Relations Between Afghanistan and the Soviet Union." *International Journal of Middle East Studies* 17 (May 1985): 151–73.

———. "The First Afghan Seven-Year Plan 1976/77–1982/83." *Afghanistan Journal* (Jg. 6, Heft 1, 1986): 15–23.

Saleh, Omar G. "Economical Geography of Afghanistan." *Afghanistan* 19 (July–September 1963): 37–43.

———. 19 (January–March 1964): 15–22.

———. 19 (April–June 1964): 37–41.

Shroder, John F. "Physical Resources and the Development of Afghanistan." *Studies in Comparative Development* 16 (Fall–Winter 1981): 36–63.

———. "Afghanistan's Unsung Riches." *Christian Science Monitor* 11 (February 1982).

———. "The USSR and Afghanistan Mineral Resources." Reprint from *International Minerals*. University of Nebraska-Omaha, Occasional Papers. no. 3, 1983, pp. 115–53.

Taussig, H. C. "Afghanistan's Agricultural Problems." *Eastern World* 20 (March–April 1966): 11–13.

U. S. Department of State. "U.S. Grants Wheat to Afghanistan to Aid Economic Development." *Department of State Bulletin* 43 (23 May 1960): 831–32.

———. "U.S. Provides Afghanistan with Another 50,000 Tons of Wheat." *Department of State Bulletin* 42 (23 May 1960): 831–32.

Ziai (Ziyaee), Hakim. "Afghanistan's Modernization." *Afghanistan* 16 (July–August–September 1963): 41–45.

Ziyaee, Hakim. "General Development of Afghanistan up to 1957." *Afghanistan* 16 (July–September 1961): 38–55.

———. "Educational Development Project Under Second Five-Year Plan and Future Long-Term Plan." *Afghanistan* 18 (October–November–December 1963): 1–22.

On Government and Politics

"About Events in Afghanistan." *Pravda*. L. Brezhnev's interview with Pravda's correspondent, 13 January 1980.

Adamec, Ludwig. "Germany, Third Power in Afghanistan's Foreign Relations." In *Afghanistan: Some New Approaches*. Ann Arbor: The University of Michigan, 1969, pp. 204–59.

"Afghanistan: 5 Years Later." *Revolutionary Workers*, 8 February 1985.

"Afghanistan's Women Lift the Veil." *New York Times Magazine*, 11 March 1956.

Ahmad, Mahfooz. "Resistance Movement in Afghanistan: 1979–81." *Pakistan Horizon Quarterly* 36 (Third Quarter 1983): 81–89.

Ahmed, Feroz. "The Khalq Failed to Comprehend the Contradictions of the Rural Sectors." *Merip Reports* 89 (July–August 1980): 13–20.

Ali, Tariq. "Afghanistan and the Consequences of Soviet Invasion." in *Can Pakistan Survive? The Death of a State*. New York: Pelican Books, 1983, pp. 164–81.

Arnold, Anthony. "The Stony Path to Afghan Socialism: Problems of Sovietization in an Alpine Muslim Society." *Orbis* 29 (Spring 1985): 40–57.

Azmi, Muhammad R. "Soviet Politico-Military Penetration in Afghanistan 1955 to 1979." *Armed Forces and Society* 12 (Spring 1986): 329–49.

Bulganin, N. A. "Speeches by N. A. Bulganin at a Dinner in Kabul, December 16, 1955." In *N. S. Khrushchev Speeches During Sojourn in India, Burma, and Afghanistan*. New Delhi: New Age Printing Press, 1956.

Canfield, Robert. "Islamic Sources of Resistance." *Orbis* 29 (Spring 1985): 57–71.

"CIA's Biggest Covert War is in Afghanistan, The." *The Washington Post National Weekly Edition*, 28 January 1985.

Dastarac, Alexander, and M. Levent. "What Went Wrong in Afghanistan." *Merip Reports* 89 (July–August 1980): 3–12.

"Did Moscow Fear an Afghan Tito?" *New York Times*, 13 January 1980.

Dupree, Louis. "Afghanistan and the Unpaved Road to Democracy." *Royal Central Asian Society Journal* 56 (October 1969): 272–78.

———. "Toward Representative Government in Afghanistan." *AUFS Reports* 14 (1978): 1–8.

———. "Inside Afghanistan: Yesterday and Today: A Strategic Appraisal." *Strategic Studies* 2 (April 1979): 64–83.

Ella, Maillart. "Afghanistan's Rebirth: An Interview with H. R. H. Hashim

Khan in 1937." *Journal of the Royal Central Asian Society* 27 (April 1940): 24.

Emadi, Hafizullah. "Afghanistan's Struggle for National Liberation." *Studies in Third World Societies* 27 (March 1984): 17–42.

———. "Resettlement Pattern: The Afghan Refugees in Pakistan." *Cultural Survival Quarterly* 12 (1988): 20–23.

Halliday, Fred. "Arc of Revolution: Iran, Afghanistan, South Yemen, Ethiopia." *Race and Class* 20 (Spring 1979): 375–90.

———. "War and Revolution in Afghanistan." *New Left Review* 119 (January–February 1980): 20–41.

Hauner, Milan. "Seizing the Third Parallel: Geopolitics and the Soviet Advance to Central Asia." *Orbis* 29 (Spring 1985): 5–31.

Herbert, C. "Afghanistan: From Coup to Anschluss." *The Army Quarterly and Defense Journal* 110 (July 1980): 285–89.

Mikhailov, K. "Provocatory Campaign over Afghanistan." *International Affairs* 3 (March 1980): 97–100.

Mir, Casim Syed. "Imperialist Design in Afghanistan: A Poisonous Tree." *Soviet Review* 17 (February 1980): 30–42.

Negaran, Hannah [pseudo name]. "Afghan Coup of 1978." *Orbis* 23 (Spring 1979): 93–114.

Olcott, Martha Brill. "Soviet Islam and World Revolution." *World Politics* 34 (July 1982): 487–504.

Rader, Ronald. "The Russian Military and Afghanistan: An Historical Perspective." In *Soviet Armed Forces Annual.* Gulf Breeze, Florida: Academic International Press, 1981, pp. 308–28.

"Resolution of the PDPA Students Association." Kabul, 1976.

Saikal, Amin. "Afghanistan and Afghan Refugees." *Current Affairs* 62 (October 1985): 14–23.

Strok, Joe. "US Involvement in Afghanistan." *Merip Reports* 8 (July–August 1980): 25–26.

"Text of Afghanistan-Pakistan Accord." *Mainichi Daily News* (Japan) 15 April 1988, p. c3.

"Text of Speech by Hafizullah Amin." *Afghanistan* 32 (June 1979): 1–35.

"Text of Speech by Noor Mohammad Taraki." *Afghanistan* 32 (June 1979): 1–4.

"Text of the Speech by President Mohammad Daoud via Radio Afghanistan." *Afghanistan* 26 (September 1973): 2–5.

"Two Kings in Check: Progress They Seek Could Undo Their Buffer States." *Wall Street Journal*, 15 March 1967.

"U. S. Needs to Keep Tighter Grip on Aid to Afghan Rebels." *Christian Science Monitor*, 24 May 1988.

"US, USSR Negotiate Afghan Pullout: Plan Reportedly Calls for Neutral Afghanistan and Pakistan." *Christian Science Monitor*, 14 February 1986.

Valenta, Jiri. "From Prague to Kabul: The Soviet Style Invasion." *International Security* 5 (Fall 1980): 114–40.

Weinbaum, Marvin G. "Afghanistan: Non-Party Parliamentary Democracy." *Journal of Developing Areas* 7 (October 1972): 57–74.

———. "Foreign Assistance to Afghan Higher Education." *Afghanistan Journal* (Jg. 3, Heft 3, 1976): 83–86.

———. "Legal Elites in Afghanistan Society." *International Journal of Middle East Studies* 12 (August 1980): 39–57.

———. "The Politics of Afghan Resettlement and Rehabilitation." *Asian Survey* 29 (March 1989): 287–307.

Yusufzai, Rahimullah. "PDPA: Khalq-Parcham Struggle for Power." *Regional Studies Quarterly* 11 (Spring 1984): 64–105.

On History

"Account by French Reporter Jean-Jose Puig." *Afghanistan Information Center Monthly Bulletin*, Peshawar: Pakistan 32–33 (November-December 1983): 27–28.

"Aims and Goals of Jamiati Islami-e-Afghanistan." *Mirror of Jihad* 1 (January-February 1982): 8–13.

Chopra, S. "Afghanistan-Pakistan Relations—The Pakhtoonistan Issue." *Indian Journal of Political Science* 35 (October-December 1974): 310–15.

Dupree, Nancy. "The Demography of Afghan Refugees in Pakistan." In *Soviet-American Relations with Pakistan, Iran and Afghanistan*. Hampshire and London: The Macmillan Press, 1987, pp. 366–94.

Eliot, Theodore L. "Afghanistan After the 1978 Revolution." *Strategic Review* 7 (Spring 1979): 57–62.

"Feuds Over CIA Aid to Afghan Rebels." *The Guardian*, 17 February 1985.

Foreign Broadcast Information Service (FBIS). *Daily Report: Middle East and Africa* 12 (12 September 1979): 3–4.

Haggerty, James. "Afghanistan the Great Games." *The Army Quarterly and Defense Journal* 110 (April 1980): 145–51.

Hangen, Welles. "Afghanistan: Progress Toward a Constitutional Monarchy and a Money Economy." *Yale Review* 6 (October 1966): 60–75.

Kakar, Hasan. "Trends in Modern Afghan History." In *Afghanistan in the 1970s*. New York: Praeger Publishers, 1974, pp. 13–33.

———. "Fall of the Afghan Monarchy in 1973." *International Journal of Middle East Studies* 9 (May 1978): 195–214.

Khalid, D. K. "Afghanistan's Struggle for National Liberation." *Internationales Asienforum* 11 (Spring 1980): 197–228.

"Living in the Past: Change Comes Slowly in Afghanistan, A Land at Asia's

Crossroads; Nation Fights Superstitions, Prejudices that Keep it Out of the Modern World." *Wall Street Journal*, 24 July 1970.

Naby, Eden. "The Changing Role of Islam as a Unifying Force in Afghanistan." In *The State, Religion, and Ethnic Politics: Afghanistan, Iran, and Pakistan*. New York: Syracuse University Press, 1986, pp. 124–54.

Patrick, Reardon J. "Modernization and Reform: The Contemporary Endeavor." In *Afghanistan: Some New Approaches*. Ann Arbor: The University of Michigan, 1969, pp. 149–203.

Poullada, Leon B. "Afghanistan and the United States: The Crucial Years." *The Middle East Journal* 35 (Spring 1981): 178–90.

Pourhadi, Ibrahim. "Afghanistan Press and Its Literary Influence 1897–1969." *Afghanistan Journal* (Jg. 3, Heft 1, 1976): 28–35.

Ramazani, R. K. "Afghanistan and the U.S.S.R." *Middle East Journal* 12 (Spring 1958): 144–52.

Roucek, Joseph S. "The Geopolitics of Afghanistan (Conditions Favorable to the Extension of Soviet Domination)." *Social Studies* 48 (April 1957): 127–29.

Rubinstein, A. Z. "Afghanistan at War." *Current History* 85 (March 1980): 117–20.

"U.S. and Third World." Central Asian Research Center. London: 15 (1985): 4.

U. S. Department of State. "Afghanistan Resistance and Soviet Occupation: A Five-Year Old Summary." *Department of State Bulletin*, Special Report, 18 (December 1984): 1–4.

———. "Afghanistan: Six Years of Soviet Occupation." *Department of State Bulletin*, Special Report, 135 (December 1985): 1–16.

Index

About the Author

HAFIZULLAH EMADI had worked for several years as a writer and reporter for the *Kabul Times Daily,* as well as for a number of other private newspapers and periodicals in Kabul, Afghanistan. Prior to the Soviet occupation of Afghanistan in December 1979, he served as a staff member in the Office of the Prime Ministry in Kabul, Afghanistan.

Emadi received his master's degree from the University of Illinois at Urbana-Champaign and his doctoral degree from the University of Hawaii-Manoa in August 1988. He is also a poet whose poems have been published in various periodicals and journals. His academic interests include the state, revolution, and developments in Third World societies.